Collector's G

POSTWAR
LIONEL
TRAINS
1945-1969

vid Doyle

©2007 David Doyle

Published by

kp krause publications
An Imprint of F+W Publications

700 East State Street • Iola, WI 54990-0001
715-445-2214 • 888-457-2873
www.krausebooks.com

Library of Congress Control Number: 2007922994
ISBN 13: 978-0-89689-541-6
ISBN 10: 0-89689-541-6

Designed by Kay Sanders
Edited by Justin Moen

Printed in China

CONTENTS

2505W Super 0 Five-Car Freight

Acknowledgments

When I worked on my first Lionel-related book, "The Standard Catalog of® Lionel Trains, 1945-1969," I had the assistance of a number of friends I had made through my years of collecting trains from that era. When I undertook this book, however, I realized that I would need to reach out for help to an even wider circle of collectors. As a result, not only has my knowledge been broadened, but so too has the circle of people that I call friends.

Many collectors and businesses shared photographs with me or allowed me to make my own images of rare and important pieces in their collections. Many knowledgeable collectors and dealers graciously reviewed the manuscript and offered corrections, criticism and commentary, and provided valuable insight on values for the items listed. Every effort has been made to present complete and accurate information here, and any errors are purely my own.

The late Gary Lavinous and his team of dedicated volunteers stayed until nearly midnight at the National Toy Train Museum helping me photograph many of the rarest pieces shown in this volume. Though their day was nearing 18 hours long, they dismantled display cases to allow access, not only without complaining, but with genuine enthusiasm.

Jan Athey, reference librarian for the Train Collector's Association, graciously located and allowed us to photograph many of Lionel's prewar catalogs. Former TCA president Dr. Paul Wassermann supplied additional images for that, and other chapters as well.

After long work days, Bill Blystone then worked well into the evening photographing items from his extensive prewar collection. Jim Nicholson allowed our photographer to spend two days in his home taking photos, then lent additional items for studio photography. With the date of the world's largest train show, the Eastern Division TCA meet in York, Pa., just around the corner—a show he runs as a volunteer—Clem Clement allowed us to photograph his wonderful Standard Gauge collection.

Barb Jones lent not only her photographic skills, but also her wonderful prewar collection and vast knowledge to this effort. Scott Douglas, another respected prewar collector, also provided photographs and information critical to this work.

The chapter on Lionel's smallest trains, and perhaps the smallest niche in prewar collecting, 00, would not have been possible without the help of Ken Shirey.

My old friend, Jeff Kane at www.ttender.com, not only sent individual items from his extensive inventory of prewar Lionel repair parts, but also many scarce 00 trains.

Dave McEntarfer contributed many photos, and much enthusiasm and experience, to this project. Joe Mania, who produces exquisite reproductions of some of Lionel's earliest, rarest and most valuable trains, provided photographs of these products as an aid in differentiating authentic pieces from reproductions. His integrity is to be commended.

Parts with Character shared much knowledge and experience with me, as well as allowing needed photos to be taken.

Barry Gilmore, who once gave the sage collecting advice, "Never buy a train you feel you should apologize for," opened his collection to our camera. Dennis Waldron answered many questions about Lionel's scale and semiscale production.

Train collecting is a passion for the entire Tschopp family, and they all pitched in on this project. Brothers Bob and John opened their collection for photography and shared their knowledge. Their sister, Mary Burns and her husband Terry put in a long, long day helping photograph the couple's fabulous prewar collection. Bob Senior provided several rare Standard Gauge pieces, and teen-ager Bobby, the newest collector of the family, tireless located trains for photography.

James D. Julia auctions provided photos of a few key pieces from their past sales.

Greg Stout of Stout Auctions, who arguably handles the largest train collections in the country, granted us unlimited access for photography, and as a result, saved many, many hours of work and miles of driving. His phenomenal knowledge and amazing memory were tremendous assets in this project.

A handful of collectors chose to remain anonymous. Their anonymity, however, does not lessen the value of their contributions of photographs and information to this work. Thank you.

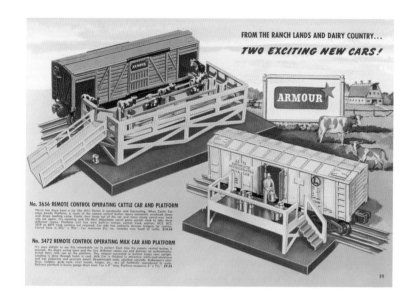

FROM THE RANCH LANDS AND DAIRY COUNTRY...

TWO EXCITING NEW CARS!

No. 3656 REMOTE CONTROL OPERATING CATTLE CAR AND PLATFORM

No. 3472 REMOTE CONTROL OPERATING MILK CAR AND PLATFORM

Lionel Trains and The

    Lionel—few brands have the instantaneous recognition this name enjoys as it begins its second century. Young or old, male or female, it seems almost everyone identifies the name with toy trains—in fact to many people the two are synonymous.

    Joshua Lionel Cohen, with Harry Grant, formed the firm on Sept. 5, 1900. Their first business was with the U.S. Navy, producing fuses for mines. Once the Navy work was completed, Cohen began tinkering, trying to find a product to keep him and his partner busy and his new firm afloat. Adapting a motor Lionel developed for a fan, a motorized gondola car was created. Provided with a circle of steel rails it was intended as an animated store window display. The year was 1901, and this was the first Lionel Electric Train.

    World War II brought a halt to Lionel's toy train production in June 1942. The Lionel plant, like countless others throughout the country, became totally devoted to manufacturing military products. WWII also brought other changes to Lionel's operations as large numbers of women joined the workforce. The complete cessation of train produc-

SECTION BY SECTION, NEVER STOPS GROWING

Create a mountain range. Use a little imagination and the No. 920 Scenic Display Set. Comes complete with paints and detailed instructions. See here as well the No. 214 Girder Bridge, No. 450 Signal Bridge and No. 494 Rotary Beacon leak!

Every line needs maintenance facilities. Such accessories as the No. 350 Transfer Table, No. 352 Icing Station, No. 195 Floodlight Tower, No. 415 Diesel Fueling Station and the No. 282 Gantry Crane are the proper components of your "equipment service" area.

A complete "Operations Control Unit" for the busy dispatcher. On this separate panel you can put everything you need for "fingertip railroading." Switch, whistle and accessory controls, microphone and locomotive throttles.

An Exciting Panorama of Railroading in a Small Space!

As your line grows, you use it take on the romance and flavor that have made "ribbons of steel" man's greatest, most fascinating form of transportation. But this need not be the end! The equipment shown here can be set up in many different ways. One of the truly great adventures of growing up is having a railroad of your own which grows with you. Only Lionel gives you a world of sturdy, true-to-life equipment with which you can add, build, change, and then add some more!

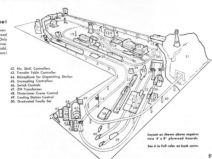

Layout as shown above requires two 4' x 8' plywood boards.

See it in full color on back cover.

51

Collecting Hobby

tion for three years provided Lionel the opportunity to completely revamp their line. When production resumed in the fall of 1945, not only was Standard-Gauge not mentioned, but the O-Gauge trains had totally new designed trucks and couplers that were incompatible with the previous models and a newly designed plastic-bodied gondola car. Over the next few years plastics would increasingly replace metals in Lionel's products.

The late 1940s and 1950s were Lionel's glory years, with the Irvington plant churning out thousands of trains in dozens of models and hundreds of paint schemes.

Some of the features Lionel trains are known for were introduced prior to WWII; die-cast boilers, electrical reversing mechanisms, dubbed "E-units," and the whistle. However, the postwar era brought about many more innovations. "Real railroad knuckle couplers" debuted in 1945, the next year smoke was added to many steam locomotives, America's favorite milk man first unloaded the milk car in 1947, the famed Santa Fe F-3 streamlined diesel took to Lionel's rails in 1948, and though untouted until 1950, in 1949 Lionel introduced Magne-traction, which magnetized the wheels of locomotives.

Ultimately, in 1969 The Lionel Toy Corp. (as it had become in 1965) exited the toy train business by licensing the name and selling the tooling to the Fundimensions Division of General Mills. Some production was moved immediately and by the mid-1970s Lionel trains were no longer a presence in the huge Hillside plant.

With the exception of 1967, Lionel Trains have been, and are still, in production every year since 1945. Today's Lionel trains have elaborate paint schemes and sophisticated electronics undreamed of during the postwar heyday.

COLLECTING

Toy train collectors are their own fraternity, eagerly welcoming new buffs with a sincere interest in toy trains. Avail yourself of this knowledge base and friendship; no matter if you are an experienced collector or a rookie, something can always be learned. There is no substitute for experience in this hobby, as in any other. No book, no matter how complete, contains all the answers. Thousands of words and the best illustrations cannot equal the experience gained by holding a piece in your own hands. There is no finer place than in the home of a friend and fellow collector. The piece that is not for sale can be examined unhurried and questions answered honestly; an excellent preparation for seeking an item in the marketplace.

The advent of Internet auctions has been a boon for collectors in remote areas. But for those in more populous areas, there is no substitute for shopping in the company of fellow collectors in hobby shops and

train shows. Examining an item personally, with the counsel of more experienced collectors, is especially urged when purchasing expensive, often repaired or forged items.

Enthusiasts have been collecting toy trains perhaps as long as they have been produced. In the United States, the largest and oldest collectors group is the Train Collectors Association, or TCA. Founded in 1954 in Yardley, Pa., the group has grown to over 31,000 members. The nationally recognized grading standards used in this volume were developed by the TCA.

The TCA headquarters is located in their Toy Train Museum and can be reached at:

The Train Collectors Association
P.O. Box 248
300 Paradise Lane
Strasburg, PA 17579
Phone: (717) 687-8623

The second-oldest organization is the Toy Train Operating Society, formed on the West Coast in 1966. The TTOS can be contacted at:

Toy Train Operating Society
25 W. Walnut Street, Suite 308
Pasadena, CA 91103
Phone: (626) 578-0673

The largest Lionel-specific club is the Lionel Collectors Club of America. The club's mailing address is:

LCCA Business Office
P.O. Box 479
La Salle, IL 61301-0479

The purpose of the Lionel Operating Train Society, or LOTS, is to provide a national club for operators (as opposed to pure collectors) of Lionel trains and accessories. LOTS can be reached at:

LOTS Business Office
6376 West Fork Road
Cincinnati, OH 45247-5704

How to Use This

This book is intended to aid both the novice and the experienced collector of Lionel products. This is an abridged version of the *"Standard Catalog of® Lionel Trains 1945-1969,"* which is more easily used at shows and flea markets. Though lacking the detail of the full-sized version, enough information is provided to differentiate between not only the primary collectable variations, but also a number of the often-forged items and authentic pieces.

This book is broken down into the following sections; Locomotives and Rolling Stock, Accessories, Cataloged Sets, and Catalogs. Within these sections, a stock number arranges the items numerically. The stock number on the vast majority of Lionel's products was stamped either on the side or underside of the item. The items are listed in numeric order in each chapter. The variations of each item are presented in chronological order, if known, or in increasing order of scarcity if the production sequence is unknown.

Thus, if you pick up a flatcar that is numbered 6467, you can turn to the flatcar section and move through the listings until you reach the number 6467. You will then find that this car was produced only in 1956 and was cataloged by Lionel as a "Miscellaneous Car." Nearby most listings you will find a photo of the item described.

For items produced over a period of years, several details must be studied to accurately date each piece. Most of these dating clues involve the trucks and couplers on the cars, or boxes they were packaged in. These changes are detailed below and a summary of these changes appears at the bottom of each page throughout the listings.

Lionel trains were built to provide a "lifetime of happiness" to quote the vintage advertising slogan; and with proper care they will do that and more. Resist the temptation to simply pull them from the attic and put them on the track or grab the first household cleanser you find to clean them with. Either of these things could cause permanent, costly damage to an otherwise fine collectable and toy.

CONDITION AND RARITY

To the collector, condition is everything. The Train Collectors Association, the world's oldest and largest train collector group, has established very precise language for describing the condition of collectable trains in order to protect both the buyer and the seller. All reputable dealers and collectors use this terminology, and in fact failure to prop-

Collector's Guide

erly use these terms in transactions between members can result in expulsion from the organization.

These grading standards are as follows:

Fair, or C4: Well-scratched, chipped, dented, rusted, warped.

Good, or C5: Small dents, scratches, dirty.

Very Good, or C6: Few scratches, exceptionally clean, no major dents or rust.

Excellent, or C7: Minute scratches or nicks, no dents or rust, all original, less than average wear.

Like New, or C8: Only the slightest signs of handling and wheel wear, brilliant colors and crisp markings; literally like new. As a rule, trains must have their original boxes in comparable condition to realize the prices listed in the grade.

Mint, or C10: Brand new, absolutely unmarred, all original and unused. Items dusty or faded from display, or with fingerprints from handling, cannot be considered mint. Although Lionel test ran their locomotives briefly at the factory, items "test run" by consumers cannot be considered mint. Most collectors expect mint items to come with all associated packaging with which they were originally supplied.

As one can imagine, Mint pieces command premium prices. The supply is extremely limited, and the demand among collectors is great, so often the billfold of the buyer, rather than a more natural supply and demand situation, limits the price of such pieces.

Demand is one of the key factors influencing values. The Santa Fe F-3 diesel was the most produced locomotive in Lionel's history, yet clean examples still command premium prices due to demand. Its classic beauty endures and essentially every enthusiast or layperson wants one.

Rarity, or scarcity, is also a factor influencing the value of trains. Low production quantities or extreme fragility cause some items to be substantially more difficult to find than others. When scarcity is coupled with demand the result is a premium price, while other items, extremely scarce, command only moderate prices due to lack of demand, or appreciation, on the part of collectors. In this guide we have rated each item on a scale of one to eight for rarity. One represents the most common items, such as the 6017 caboose, while eight is assigned to those items hardest to find, such as the gray 3562-1 barrel car with red lettering. It is hoped that this rarity rating will help the collector when having to choose which of the similar priced items to buy by answering the proverbial "How likely am I to get this chance again?" question.

Supply, as a short-term extension of rarity, whether actual or temporary, also affects price. If only one sought after item is at a given show, the seller is unlikely to negotiate or reduce his price. If however multiple sellers at a given event have identical items, no matter how rare, the temporary market glut can bring about temporarily reduced prices.

Lastly, the **buyer's intent** will effect what they are willing to pay. A collector who intends to add a piece to their permanent collection will obviously pay more for an item than a dealer who is intending to resell the item will pay for the same item.

Prices are given in this guide for trains in Very Good, Excellent and Like New condition. Trains in less than Very Good condition are not generally considered collectable, and as mentioned earlier, Mint condition trains are too uncommon to establish pricing on.

The prices listed are what a group of collectors would consider a reasonable price to pay to add that piece to their collection. When contemplating a sale to a dealer, you should expect to receive 30 to 50 percent less than the listed values, with the poorer condition the trains the greater the amount of discount, due to the greater difficulty the dealer will have selling them. Remember that these prices are only a guideline. You are spending your money, what an item is worth to you is of greater importance than what it is worth to the author. Conversely, the publisher does not sell trains, this is not a mail-order catalog, and you should not expect a dealer or collector to "price match."

AIDS TO DATING TRAINS

Unlike certain other collectibles, the age of a Lionel train is not a factor in its value. That is, an older train is not inherently more valuable than a newer train. It is rather the variations in construction throughout an item's production run that effect its scarcity, and thus value. Many Lionel trains are marked on the sides with "New" or "Built" dates. These dates are totally irrelevant to when a piece was actually produced, and are decorative only. During the mid-1950s, Lionel added the year introduced as a prefix or suffix to the stock number of some cars, such as the 336155 markings on the log dump cars introduced in 1955, or the 546446 N & W hopper car from 1954, but this was not universally done.

Although a few collectors specialize in a specific year or two of Lionel production, they are the exception as opposed to the rule. Instead, most collectors establish the production date of these trains, or when trying to properly and precisely re-create a given train set.

Among the key aids to dating trains are the construction techniques used in the manufacture of the trucks and couplers, and the type of original packaging used, if still present.

LIONEL FREIGHT TRUCKS

The trucks that collectors refer to as **"staple-end"** are so named because the end of the bolster (the upper crosspiece of a truck, which serves as its attachment point to the railroad car) has been staked to secure the zinc side frames. The staking resembles a folded staple, thus the moniker.

Staple-end Truck

These so-called staple-end trucks were used from 1945 until 1951.

In 1951, the staple-end trucks were superceded by what collectors refer to as **"bar-end"** trucks. The earlier design allowed with time the side frames to loosen from the bolster. The improved design featured the side frames being forced down onto the bolster. Thus, the end of the bolster visible to the observer remains smooth, and looks like a steel bar. This truck was the mainstay of Lionel's freight car production until 1961, when it was largely phased out until 1969, when it reappeared on selected better items.

Bar-end Truck

The **"Scout"** truck was introduced in 1948, along with its associated coupler, as a low-cost component of these low cost sets. The bolster and side frame supports were a single piece of stamped

Scout Truck

steel, with the side frames being separate pieces of plastic attached to the sheet metal. While the scout coupler was discontinued in 1951 because it was incompatible with the normal Lionel coupler, the truck itself lingered until 1953 before being phased out, being equipped in its twilight years with standard magnetic couplers.

In 1957, Lionel introduced their new plastic truck. Molded of Delrin, a self-lubricating plastic, the detailed trucks were styled after a real railroad truck developed by the Association of American Railroads **(AAR)**, and bore the tiny raised word **"Timken"** on the ends of the simulated journals.

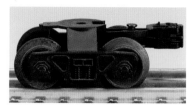

"Timken" Truck

Archbar trucks were introduced in 1959 to equip the new line of 19th century-style trains pulled by the "General" steam locomotive inspired by Disney's "Great Locomotive Chase" movie. These

Archbar Truck

trucks, like the AAR trucks, were molded plastic, and though very different cosmetically from the AAR trucks, were almost identical from the manufacturing standpoint.

LIONEL BOXES

The box that most often comes to the mind's eye when thinking Lionel trains is the traditional orange and blue box. However, from 1945 through 1969 Lionel used no less than 15 types of boxes for their rolling stock. The changes in the boxes can be an aid to dating trains known to be in their original packages, such as those purchased from their original owner or found in an attic. Beware, however that many unknowing (or uncaring) collectors and dealers often place items in the improper vintage box in an effort to "upgrade" the packaging.

Early Postwar: The original boxes used for individual cars and

Early Postwar

small accessories in the postwar era had bold blue lettering that touched the tops and bottoms of the blue lettering frames and outlines. This box was used from 1945 through 1947; the 1947 boxes are distinguished by the logo of the Toy Manufacturer's Association.

First Traditional: The most remembered box of the post-war era was introduced in 1948. The names of cities with Lionel showrooms: "NEW YORK," "CHICAGO" and "SAN FRAN-CISCO" were imprinted inside borders on the sides of the box. The stock number of the box contents was printed on all four sides of the box, as well as on the end flaps.

First Traditional

Middle Traditional: This box is the same as Early Traditional, except the city name "SAN FRANCISCO" was eliminated, reflecting the closure of the West Coast sales office. This box was in use from mid-1949 through 1955. However, the 1955 boxes were considerably redesigned. The heavy corrugated cardboard liners that previously had been used inside of many of the boxes, particularly locomotives, were eliminated, and the boxes downsized accordingly.

Middle Traditional

OPS Traditional: This box was the same as the Middle Traditional, but was factory printed with a Korean War-era OPS (Office of Price Stabilization) price. This box was used in 1952. As an aside, Lionel pro-

OPS Traditional

vided dealers with sheets of adhesive backed white OPS stickers for application to older items already in stock.

Late Traditional: This box is the same as the Middle Traditional, but for the removal of the stock number from the four sides, leaving it only on the ends. This box was introduced in 1956 and used through 1958.

Late Traditional

Bold Traditional: The Bold Traditional box is an uncommon box similar to the Late Traditional box, but had much bolder typeface print on the end flaps. This box was only used in 1958, and then only for part of the product line.

Bold Traditional

Glossy: In 1958, a few boxes were made of smooth glossy coated cardstock. This box is very uncommon.

Perforated: By 1959, merchandising trends had moved toward consumer self-service, and Lionel's products had an increasing presence in discount chains. This resulted in a total change in Lionel's packaging. The new box was made of orange coated stock and featured a tear-out perforated front panel that allowed the contents to be displayed. This box was introduced in 1959 and used through 1960.

Glossy

Perforated

Orange Picture: This box, also made of glossy orange cardstock, had a white panel with an illustration of a steam and diesel locomotive on the front. The city names "NEW YORK" and "CHICAGO" appeared on the box, as did the corporate name "THE LIONEL CORPORATION." This is the box that was in use from 1961 through 1964.

Perforated Picture: In 1961 and 1962, boxes were occasionally produced that featured an illustrated white front panel which also was perforated for removal.

Hillside Picture: Essentially the same as the Orange Picture, but rather than the showroom locations of New York and Chicago, the box sides bore "HILLSIDE, N.J.," (the location of Lionel's factory) and bore the new corporate name "THE LIONEL TOY CORPORATION." This box was used for part of 1965.

Window Box: Furthering the idea introduced with 1958's perforated box, in 1966, Lionel introduced the window box. With this box the contents were still visible through a cellophane window in the front of the box, but yet were protected from shop wear and dust. Today this car is often found with cellophane loose or missing. The boxes were more generic than their predecessors, with the stock number being rubber stamped according to contents, rather than being machine printed during the box's manufacturing process.

Orange Picture

Hillside Picture

Window Box

Hagerstown Checkerboard: In 1968, the boxes were revised yet again. Now the boxes featured a bold white and orange checkerboard pattern. Yet again, the city imprint changed as well, this time to "HAGERSTOWN, MARYLAND," reflecting Lionel's 1967 relocation

Hagerstown Checkerboard

of manufacturing operations to the Hagerstown facility of their Porter science subsidiary. Unlike the custom packaging of the 50s, one size of Checkerboard box was used for the vast majority of the rolling stock. In most cases the stock numbers were rubber stamped on boxes.

Hillside Checkerboard: Lionel returned to Hillside, N.J. in 1969, and so of course the boxes reflected the move. Other than the city imprint, the Hillside Checkerboard boxes were the same as the Checkerboard.

Generic: During the final days of the postwar era, from time to time Lionel resorted to using plain white boxes with stock numbers rubber stamped, or occasionally type stamped on the end flaps.

HOW TO USE THIS COLLECTOR'S GUIDE

REFERENCE EXAMPLE

1. ⟶

2. ⟶ **2350 (Type III)**: While difficult to locate, the version with white
3. ⟶ "N," orange "H," white "NEW HAVEN," as well as painted nose
markings, is not as sought after as the two versions listed above.

4. ⟶

VG	Ex	LN	Rarity
500	800	1,300	6

A.   B.   C.   D.

1.) **Photo:** In some listings, photos are supplied to better help identify and verify what Model and Type you possess.
2.) **Listing Name/Type:** Items will be listed by Model number and Variation number (Type).
3.) **Listing Description:** Located directly after the Listing Name/Type is a brief description of the listing, giving vital information to better help identification.
4.) **Values Table:** Below the Listing Description is the Values Table. Values for each condition are in U.S. Dollars.
    A.) VG=*Very Good:* Few scratches, exceptionally clean, no major dents or rust, also known as C6.
    B.) EX=*Excellent:* Minute scratches or nicks, no dents or rust, all original, less than average wear, now known as C7.
    C.) LN=*Like New:* Only the slightest signs of handling and wheel wear, brilliant colors and crisp markings; literally like new, or C8. As a rule, Like New trains must have their original boxes in comparable condition to realize the prices listed in this guide.
    D.) Rarity: On a scale of 1-8, this system will assess the accessibility and rarity of the particular listing. On occasion, an item may be so rare that there is not enough reference to place a price or rarity.

Postwar Locomotives

Ask anyone on the street, "What do you remember about a Lionel train?" and most of them will smile as fond memories return and say, "It's black, heavy, and you put little pills in the smoke stack." This is a fitting description for the bulk of Lionel's postwar steamers.

Lionel had introduced zinc-alloy die-casting in its manufacturing processes prior to World War II, though it took a few years to perfect. Impurities in the metal can cause it to "rot" over years, swelling and disintegrating—a common problem in prewar trains, but unusual in postwar production. This new process allowed the company to create handsome, detailed, yet rugged locomotives. The mechanisms housed in these heavy metal boiler shells were works of art themselves, especially during the late 1940s when they were as precisely made as a fine watch. Ultimately, some of the less-expensive locomotives came to be made of plastic, but die-casting remained the basis for the better engines until the end. Continued innovation kept Lionel ahead of its competition, and the steam locomotives were at the forefront. Prior to World War II, Lionel had introduced its famed air whistle. Usually housed inside the tender, a small electric motor turned an impeller, forcing air through two acoustic chambers and producing a realistic whistle sound. The motor was controlled by a relay, which was closed by imposing

and Rolling Stock

a slight DC current on top of the normal AC track power that ran the train. A similar relay was used to ring the bell on the switch engines.

In 1946, Lionel wooed consumers by producing the first locomotives with puffing smoke. These were replicas of a handsome 2-8-4 Berkshire and Pennsylvania's revolutionary, albeit unsuccessful, S-2 turbine. The first year's smoke unit used a special oversized light bulb to heat the smoke material, but beginning in 1947 a nichrome wire-wound heater element was used instead on most of the larger locomotives. It was these units that seemed to have an insatiable appetite for the memorable "SP" smoke pellets. In the late 1950s, a third type of smoke generator appeared that used a liquid rather than pills.

Lionel's golden anniversary year of 1950 saw the final major innovation in steam locomotive production—the introduction of Magnetraction. This feature was intended to better keep the locomotive on the track and increase its pulling power by using powerful Alnico magnets to magnetize the wheel, "sticking" the train to Lionel's tin-plated steel track. The fortunes of Lionel seemed to parallel that of full-size steam locomotives. Both reached their zenith in the late 1940s and early 1950s, and both seemed to be fading memories by the late 1960s.

42 Picatinny Arsenal Switcher

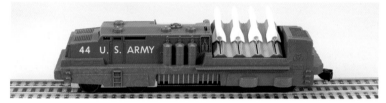

44 U.S. Army Mobile Missile Launcher

53 Rio Grande Switcher (Type I)

56 M St. L Switcher

	VG	EX	LN	RARITY
41 UNITED STATES ARMY SWITCHER: 1955-57, painted.	125	160	200	3
Unpainted black body.	200	300	425	5
42 PICATINNY ARSENAL SWITCHER: 1957, unpainted olive drab body.	200	300	425	5
44 U.S. ARMY MOBILE MISSILE LAUNCHER: 1959-62, painted blue body.	150	250	325	5
45 U.S. MARINES MOBILE MISSILE LAUNCHER: 1960-62, painted olive drab.	175	275	425	6
50 LIONEL GANG CAR: 1954-64, gray (1954) two-piece horn.	375	500	675	7
Blue bumpers, two-piece horn.	50	75	125	4
Blue bumpers, one-piece horn.	40	60	75	2
51 NAVY YARD NEW YORK SWITCHER: 1956-57, unpainted blue plastic body.	125	175	250	4
52 FIRE CAR: 1958-61, red-painted black plastic body.	125	200	300	5
53 RIO GRANDE SWITCHER: 1957-60, with plow "a" in Rio Grande printed normally.	425	600	950	8
"a" in Rio Grande reversed (prototypically correct).	225	325	475	6
54 BALLAST TAMPER: 1958-61, 1966-69, unpainted yellow plastic body.	150	225	325	5
55 TIE-JECTOR: 1957-61.	150	225	325	5
56 M St. L SWITCHER: 1958, body painted red, cab sides painted white.	300	550	850	6
57 AEC SWITCHER: 1959-60, unpainted white body, cab sides painted red.	450	700	1,250	7
58 GREAT NORTHERN SWITCHER/ SNOWPLOW: 1959-1961, unpainted green plastic with white cab sides equipped with a rotary snow blower.	300	500	850	5
59 U.S. AIR FORCE MINUTEMAN SWITCHER: 1961-63, unpainted white body.	300	500	775	5
60 LIONELVILLE RAPID TRANSIT TROLLEY: 1955-58, yellow body, red roof.				
Black lettering, no vents and metal motorman silhouettes.	200	300	425	5
Black lettering, no vents and no motorman silhouettes.	150	275	350	4
Blue lettering, no vents and no motormen.	100	175	250	3

65 Handcar

69 Maintenance Car

209 New Haven Alco A-A

212(T) United States Marine Corps Alco A Dummy

	VG	EX	LN	RARITY
Blue lettering, no motormen, with vents.	150	225	325	4

65 HANDCAR: 1962-66, molded.

	VG	EX	LN	RARITY
Light yellow plastic body.	200	400	600	5
Dark yellow plastic body.	175	325	500	4
Strengthened body molding.	225	450	650	6
68 EXECUTIVE INSPECTION CAR: 1958-61, gray plastic, painted red and cream.	175	300	425	4
69 MAINTENANCE CAR: 1960-62, dark gray brushplate, black body, both unpainted.	225	350	500	5
202 UNION PACIFIC ALCO A: 1957, painted orange.	75	100	150	2
204 SANTA FE ALCO A-A: 1957, powered and dummy painted blue and yellow. Dummy has operating headlight.	100	175	275	4
205 MISSOURI PACIFIC ALCO A-A: 1957-58, painted solid blue with factory installed steel nose supports.	100	175	275	5
Without factory installed steel nose supports painted to match.	75	150	250	4
208 SANTA FE ALCO A-A: 1958-59, painted blue and yellow, no headlight in dummy.	75	150	250	4
209 NEW HAVEN ALCO A-A: 1958 only, black, white and orange paint on molded black plastic body.	400	600	1,100	6
210 TEXAS SPECIAL ALCO A-A: 1958 only, painted red and white body.	75	150	250	4
211 TEXAS SPECIAL ALCO A-A: 1962-63, 1965-66, cosmetically almost identical to the 210.	75	150	250	5
212 SANTA FE ALCO A-A: 1964-66, painted red and silver. Some stamped "BLT/BY LIONEL." Others were stamped "BLT 8-57/BY LIONEL," but no difference in value or scarcity.	100	175	275	4
212 UNITED STATES MARINE CORPS ALCO A: 1958-59, painted dark blue.	100	175	250	4
Painted medium blue.	150	225	325	6
212(T) UNITED STATES MARINE CORPS ALCO A DUMMY: 1958, painted medium blue body.	450	675	1,200	7
213 MINNEAPOLIS & ST. LOUIS ALCO A-A: 1964, painted red.	125	225	325	5

215 SANTA FE ALCO: 1965-66, painted red and silver.

	VG	EX	LN	RARITY
A-A with 212T.	90	150	250	3

216 Burlington Alco A

221 Santa Fe Alco A

221 United States Marine Corps Alco A

224 United States Navy Alco A-B

	VG	EX	LN	RARITY
A-B with 218C.	100	175	275	4
216 BURLINGTON ALCO A: 1958, painted silver and red.	200	350	450	6
216 MINNEAPOLIS & ST. LOUIS ALCO A: 1965, painted red body, came as single A-unit.	100	150	200	4
A-A combination with 213T.	175	225	350	5
217 B & M ALCO A-B: 1959, unpainted blue plastic bodies with the roof and A-unit nose painted black.	90	165	250	5
218 SANTA FE ALCO: 1959-63, painted silver and red, A-A, normal nose decal.	100	150	225	3
A-A solid yellow nose decals that lacked the red areas inside the perimeter.	125	175	275	5
A-B combination (1961).	100	150	250	4
218C SANTA FE ALCO B-UNIT: 1961-63, painted silver.	50	75	115	4
219 MISSOURI PACIFIC ALCO A-A: 1959 only, uncataloged blue-painted pair.	100	175	290	5
220 SANTA FE ALCO: 1960-61, painted silver and red, A only.	75	125	175	3
A-A combination.	150	225	300	3
221 2-6-4 STEAM: 1946-47, painted either 221T or 221W tender with gray silver wheels.	100	150	200	4
Gray, black wheels.	75	100	150	3
Black, black wheels.	50	75	125	2
221 RIO GRANDE ALCO A: 1963-64, unpainted yellow body.	40	70	90	2
221 SANTA FE ALCO A: 1964, uncataloged, unpainted olive drab body, no E-unit, wired for forward-only travel.	250	500	800	7
221 UNITED STATES MARINE CORPS ALCO A: 1964, uncataloged, unpainted olive drab body.	225	375	600	6
222 RIO GRANDE ALCO A: 1962, painted yellow, wired to run forward only.	50	75	100	2
223 SANTA FE ALCO A-B: 1963, painted silver and red.	125	200	325	5
224 2-6-2 STEAM: 1945-46, with 2466W or 2466WX tender.				
1945: without tender drawbar, black railings, squared cab floor.	75	125	225	4
1946: with tender drawbar, silver railings, rounded cab floor.	60	100	150	2
224 UNITED STATES NAVY ALCO A-B: 1960 only, painted blue.	150	225	350	6

229 Minneapolis & St. Louis Alco

231 Rock Island Alco A

235 2-4-2 Steam

240 2-4-2 Steam

	VG	EX	LN	RARITY
225 CHESAPEAKE & OHIO ALCO A: 1960 only, painted dark blue.	75	125	175	4
226 B & M ALCO A-B: 1960 only, B-unit always unpainted blue plastic.				
A-unit unpainted blue.	100	175	275	5
A-unit painted blue.	150	225	325	6
227 CANADIAN NATIONAL ALCO A: 1960 only, molded gray body painted green.	100	150	200	5
228 CANADIAN NATIONAL ALCO A: 1960 only, uncataloged, body painted green.	100	150	200	6
229 MINNEAPOLIS & ST. LOUIS ALCO: 1961-62.				
Single A.	75	100	150	4
A-B combination.	125	175	275	5
230 CHESAPEAKE & OHIO ALCO A: 1961 only, painted dark blue.	75	125	175	3
231 ROCK ISLAND ALCO A: 1961-63, painted black with white heat-stamped lettering and a white roofline stripe.				
With broad red stripe.	75	125	175	5
Without broad red stripe.	225	375	500	7
232 NEW HAVEN ALCO A: 1962, painted overall orange with two narrow black stripes.	75	125	175	5
233 2-4-2 STEAM: 1961-62, with 233W tender.	50	75	125	4
235 2-4-2 STEAM: 1961, supplied with either the 1050T or 1130T tender.	150	250	375	7
236 2-4-2 STEAM: 1961-62, supplied with either the 1050T or 1130T tender.	20	35	50	2
237 2-4-2 STEAM: 1963-66, thick or thin running boards, 1061T, 1062T, 242T or 1060T tender small streamlined.	30	50	85	2
234W: Whistle tender, 1965-66.	60	100	175	3
238 2-4-2 STEAM: 1963-64, furnished with the 234W whistle tender. Thick or thin running boards.	100	150	250	5
239 2-4-2 STEAM: 1965-66, came with either 242T or 234W tender, add $50 premium for 234W.				
Cab number heat stamped.	25	45	70	3
Cab number rubber stamped.	40	75	100	3
240 2-4-2 STEAM: 1964, uncataloged, came with 242T tender.	150	225	400	7

251 2-4-2 Steam

600 MKT (gray frame, yellow platform railings, blued steel steps)

600 MKT (gray frame, blued steel railings and steps)

600 MKT (black frame, blued steel railings and steps)

	VG	EX	LN	RARITY
241 2-4-2 STEAM: 1965-66, uncataloged, with 234W tender.				
Painted white stripe.	100	175	275	5
Rubber-stamped white stripe.	90	150	240	5
242 2-4-2 STEAM: 1962-66, came with 242T, 1060T, 1061T or 1062T tender.	10	20	40	1
243 2-4-2 STEAM: 1960 only, came with the 243W tender.	70	100	200	4
244 2-4-2 STEAM: 1960-61, came with either 244T or 1130T tender.	25	35	50	2
245 2-4-2 STEAM: 1959, uncataloged, came with 1130T tender.	40	70	90	3
246 2-4-2 STEAM: 1959-61, came with either the 1130T or the 244T tender.	20	30	40	2
247 2-4-2 STEAM: 1959 only, with 247T tender, with matching blue stripe.	45	65	100	3
248 2-4-2 STEAM: 1958, uncataloged, with 1130T.	60	70	85	4
249 2-4-2 STEAM: 1958 only, with 250T tender with matching red stripe.	25	45	65	3
250 2-4-2 STEAM: 1957 only, with 250T tender with matching red stripe.	25	40	50	3
251 2-4-2 STEAM: 1966 only, with 1062T tender.	150	200	375	7
400 BALTIMORE & OHIO RDC-1: 1956-58.	125	225	325	3
404 BALTIMORE & OHIO RDC-4: 1957-58.	200	300	425	4
520 LIONEL LINES 1-B-0 ELECTRIC: 1956-57, unpainted red plastic body, black plastic pantograph.	75	120	175	3
Copper-colored plastic pantograph.	100	130	225	4
600 M K T NW-2: 1955, unpainted red plastic body.				
Gray frame, yellow platform railings, blued steel steps.	375	550	850	6
Gray frame, blued steel railings and steps.	275	425	650	5
Black frame, blued steel railings and steps.	125	175	250	4
Blued steel frame, blued steel railings and steps.	115	160	225	3
601 SEABOARD NW-2: 1956, painted black and red.	100	150	225	3

610 Erie NW-2

614 Alaska Railroad NW-2

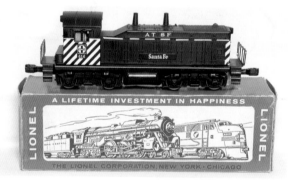

616 Santa Fe NW-2

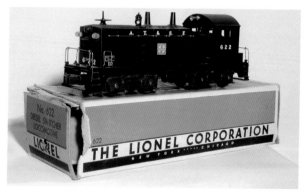

622 A. T. & S. F. NW-2

	VG	EX	LN	RARITY
602 SEABOARD NW-2: 1957-58, painted black and red.	125	175	250	3
610 ERIE NW-2: 1955 only, body painted black, yellow heat-stamped number.				
Yellow frame and platform railings, blued steel steps.	425	650	1,200	7
Black frame, blued steel railings and steps.	125	175	250	4
Blued steel frame, blued steel railings and steps.	100	150	225	3
611 JERSEY CENTRAL NW-2: 1957-58, blue and orange body.				
Unpainted deep blue body.	150	225	350	3
Unpainted light blue body.	150	225	350	3
Painted blue body.	400	600	950	6
613 UNION PACIFIC NW-2: 1958 only, yellow and gray.	250	400	600	6
614 ALASKA RAILROAD NW-2: 1959-60.				
"BUILT BY/LIONEL" outlined in yellow.	325	475	800	7
"BUILT BY/LIONEL" unpainted.	150	225	300	4
616 SANTA FE NW-2: 1961-62, painted black with white safety stripes.				
Open but unused E-unit and bell slots.	125	175	250	4
Plugged E-unit slot and open bell slot.	200	325	475	6
Both E-unit and bell slots plugged.	200	325	475	6
617 SANTA FE NW-2: 1963, painted black with white safety stripes. Came with black ornamental bell, silver ornamental horn, head and marker light lenses, and radio antenna.	150	250	375	6
621 JERSEY CENTRAL NW-2: 1956-57, unpainted blue plastic body.	100	150	200	3
622 A. T. & S. F. NW-2: 1949-50, black, die-cast frame.				
With "622" stamped on the nose of the locomotive.	200	325	525	6
Without "622" stamped on the nose of the locomotive.	150	200	350	3

626 Baltimore and Ohio Center Cab

629 Burlington Center Cab

637 2-6-4 Steam

645 Union Pacific NW-2

	VG	EX	LN	RARITY
623 A. T. & S. F. NW-2: 1952-54, black, die-cast frame.				
Hood-side handrail retained by 10 stanchions.	125	175	250	4
Hood-side handrail retained by three stanchions.	100	150	225	3
624 CHESAPEAKE & OHIO NW-2: 1952-54, medium blue, die-cast frame.				
Hood-side handrail retained by 10 stanchions.	150	250	400	5
Hood-side handrail retained by three stanchions.	150	225	375	4
Painted light blue.	300	450	700	7
625 LEHIGH VALLEY CENTER CAB: 1957-58, unpainted red body.	100	175	225	4
626 BALTIMORE AND OHIO CENTER CAB: 1956-57, unpainted blue body.	250	400	625	6
627 LEHIGH VALLEY CENTER CAB: 1956-57, unpainted red plastic body.	65	115	150	2
628 NORTHERN PACIFIC CENTER CAB: 1956-57, unpainted black body.	100	150	225	4
629 BURLINGTON CENTER CAB: 1956, silver painted body.	250	450	850	7
633 SANTA FE NW-2: 1962, painted blue body with yellow safety stripes.	125	200	300	5
634 SANTA FE NW-2: 1963, 1965-66, painted blue body.				
Yellow safety stripes, 1963.	125	175	250	4
No stripes, 1965-66.	75	125	200	3
635 UNION PACIFIC NW-2: 1965 only, painted yellow body.	75	125	200	5
637 2-6-4 STEAM: 1959-61, with 2046W or 736W tenders.				
Number rubber stamped.	75	125	200	4
Number heat stamped.	120	175	300	5
638-2361 STOKELY-VAN CAMP'S BOXCAR: 1962-64, uncataloged.	20	40	60	5
645 UNION PACIFIC NW-2: 1969, unpainted yellow plastic body.	75	125	200	4
646 4-6-4 STEAM: 1954-58, came with 2046W tenders, silver or white cab lettering.	175	250	350	4

671 6-8-6 Steam

671RR 6-8-6 Steam

682 6-8-6 Steam

685 4-6-4 Steam

	VG	EX	LN	RARITY
665 4-6-4 STEAM: 1954-56, 1966, with 6026W, 2046W or 736W tender. Rubber- or heat-stamped numbers on loco.	150	250	300	3
671 6-8-6 STEAM: 1946-49, 1946, locos have bulb-type smoke units, heater units used thereafter. Came with 671W or 2671W tenders, $50-75 premium for the latter.				
"6200" stamped in white on boiler front.	175	225	325	4
"6200" decal.	135	175	275	3
With 2671W tender, with backup lights.	325	475	650	7
671R 6-8-6 STEAM: 1946-49, "Electronic Control."				
Bulb-type smoke unit.	250	350	500	7
Heater-type smoke unit.	225	325	425	6
671RR 6-8-6 STEAM: 1952 only, came with 2046W-50 tender.				
Without "RR" suffix stamped on cab.	185	275	375	5
With "RR" suffix stamped on cab.	225	350	475	6
675 2-6-2 STEAM: 1947-49, with 2466WX or 6466WX tender.				
White "675" stamped on boiler front.	125	175	250	5
Red keystone decal on boiler front.	85	145	225	2
675 2-6-4 STEAM: 1952 only, with 2046W tender.	85	145	225	3
681 6-8-6 STEAM: 1950-51, 1953.				
1950-51: 2671W, loco number stamped in silver.	160	275	375	3
1953: 2046W-50, tender loco number stamped in white.	150	250	350	4
682 6-8-6 STEAM: 1954-55, came with a 2046W-50 tender.	275	425	650	5
685 4-6-4 STEAM: 1953 only, came with 6026W tender.				
Rubber numbers.	250	350	550	6
Heat-stamped numbers.	200	300	400	5

726 2-8-4 Steam

736 2-8-4 Steam

746 4-8-4 Steam

773 4-6-4 Steam

	VG	EX	LN	RARITY
726 2-8-4 STEAM: 1946-49, with 2426W tender.				
1946: bulb-type smoke units.	300	475	600	5
1947-49: heater-type smoke unit.	225	350	475	4
726RR 2-8-4 STEAM: 1952 only, came with 2046W tender.				
Without "RR" suffix stamped on cab.	225	375	475	4
With "RR" suffix stamped on cab.	300	425	600	5
736 2-8-4 STEAM: 1950-51, 1953-68, with 2671WX.	300	425	575	4
With 2046W or 736W tender.	200	300	400	4
746 4-8-4 STEAM: 1957-60.				
Short-striped 746W without number stamping.	600	850	1,100	5
Long-striped tender stamped 746W.	650	900	1,400	6
773 4-6-4 STEAM: 1950, with 2426W tender.	900	1,200	1,900	6
1964: with Pennsy 736W tender.	600	850	1,200	4
1964-66: with 773W NYC tender.	725	900	1,500	4
1001 2-4-2 STEAM: 1948 only, all with 1001T tender.				
Plastic boiler, silver numbers.	90	125	175	6
Plastic boiler, white numbers.	25	40	60	2
Die-cast boiler.	225	325	450	7
1002 LIONEL GONDOLA: 1948-52.				
Black or blue.	7	10	15	1
Red, silver or yellow.	225	375	500	5
X1004 BABY RUTH BOXCAR: 1948-52, outline or solid lettering.	6	10	14	1
1005 SUNOCO TANK CAR: 1948-50, gray tank.				
Medium blue lettering.	5	7	12	1
Dark blue lettering.	5	7	12	2

1007 Lionel Lines Caboose

1050 0-4-0 Steam

1061 2-4-2 Steam

1065 Union Pacific Alco A

	VG	EX	LN	RARITY
1007 LIONEL LINES CABOOSE: 1948-52.				
Red body.	2	4	6	2
Tuscan body.	75	200	300	7
1050 0-4-0 STEAM: 1959 only, came with a 1050T slope-back tender.	150	200	350	6
1055 TEXAS SPECIAL ALCO A: 1959-60, painted red with white lettering.	40	60	90	2
1060 2-4-2 STEAM: 1960-62, came with 1050T or 1060T tender, long or short rain shield over loco headlight.	10	25	50	1
1061 0-4-0 or 2-4-2 STEAM: 1963-64, 1969 used 1061T, 1062T, 1060T or 242T tenders.				
White heat-stamped cab numbers.	10	25	45	1
No cab numbers.	110	200	250	5
Cab numbers on paper label.	150	225	300	7
1062 0-4-0 or 2-4-2 STEAM: 1963-64, used 1061T, 1062T, 1060T or 242T tenders.				
With Lionel Lines or undecorated tender.	10	20	35	1
With Southern Pacific tender.	95	125	175	6
1065 UNION PACIFIC ALCO A: 1961 only, body painted yellow.	45	65	100	2
1066 UNION PACIFIC ALCO A: 1964, uncataloged unpainted yellow body.	45	65	100	2
1101 2-4-2 STEAM: 1948 only, with 1001T tender.	15	35	55	3
1110 2-4-2 STEAM: 1949, 1951-52, with 1001T tender.				
Baldwin disc drive wheels.	25	40	60	3
Spoke drive wheels.	10	20	35	1
1120 2-4-2 STEAM: 1950 only, with 1001T tender.	15	30	50	2
1130 2-4-2 STEAM: 1953-54, with 6066T or 1130T tender.				
Die-cast boiler.	225	350	450	7
Plastic boiler, silver rubber-stamped numbers.	10	25	40	3
Plastic boiler, white heat-stamped numbers.	30	70	100	5

1625 0-4-0 Steam

1665 0-4-0 Seam

1872 4-4-0 Steam

1875 Western & Atlantic Coach

	VG	EX	LN	RARITY
1615 0-4-0 STEAM: 1955-57, with 1615T tender.	125	175	275	3
1625 0-4-0 STEAM: 1958 only, with 1625T tender.	175	275	425	6
1654 2-4-2 STEAM: 1946-47.				
With 1654T tender.	30	50	70	3
With 1654W tender.	35	60	95	3
1655 2-4-2 STEAM: 1948-49, with 6654W tender.	40	70	100	3
1656 0-4-0 STEAM: 1948-49, with 6403B tender.				
Separate Bakelite coal pile.	225	350	500	6
Integral die-cast coal pile.	200	300	450	5
1665 0-4-0 STEAM: 1946 only, with 2403B tender.				
Heat-stamped tender lettering.	200	325	475	5
Rubber-stamped tender lettering.	250	375	525	6
1666 2-6-2 STEAM: 1946-47.				
Number plate beneath cab window.	60	100	175	3
Number rubber stamped beneath cab window.	100	150	250	5
1862 4-4-0 STEAM: 1959-62, with 1862T tender.	125	200	300	3
1865 WESTERN & ATLANTIC COACH: 1959-62, body painted yellow with brown roof.	20	30	40	3
1866 WESTERN & ATLANTIC MAIL-BAGGAGE: 1959-62, body painted yellow with brown roof.	20	30	40	3
1872 4-4-0 STEAM: 1959-62, with 1872T tender.	150	250	350	4
1875 WESTERN & ATLANTIC COACH: 1959-62, body painted yellow with brown roof.	125	200	275	5
1875W WESTERN & ATLANTIC COACH WITH WHISTLE: 1959-62, body painted yellow with brown roof.	60	100	150	3
1876 WESTERN & ATLANTIC MAIL-BAGGAGE: 1959-62, body painted yellow with brown roof.	40	65	90	3

1882 4-4-0 Steam

1885 Western & Atlantic Coach

2020 6-8-6 Steam

2023 Union Pacific Alco A-A

	VG	EX	LN	RARITY
1877 FLATCAR: 1959-62, unpainted brown plastic, came with a load of two white, two tan and brown, and two black horses made by Bachmann Bros. (hence the "BB" logo on the horses' bellies), and a 10-section maroon fence.	30	75	110	4
1882 4-4-0 STEAM: 1960 only, came with 1882T tender.	425	550	900	7
1885 WESTERN & ATLANTIC COACH: 1960, painted blue with brown roof.	175	250	350	6
1887 FLATCAR: 1960 only, unpainted brown plastic, came with a load of two white, two tan and brown, and two black horses made by Bachmann Bros. (hence the "BB" logo on the horses' bellies), and a 10-section fence.	140	200	275	6
2016 2-6-4 STEAM: 1955-56, with 6026W tender.				
Number heat stamped.	75	100	175	3
Number rubber stamped.	150	250	350	5
2018 2-6-4 STEAM: 1956-59.				
With 6026T or 1130T tender.	50	65	100	2
With 6026W tender.	65	100	150	2
2020 6-8-6 STEAM: 1946-49, 1946 locos have bulb-type smoke units, heater units used thereafter; "6200" stamped in white on some boiler fronts, decaled on most, came with 2020W or 6020W tender.				
"6200" stamped in white on boiler front.	175	225	350	4
"6200" decal.	150	225	285	3
With heater-type smoke unit.	165	225	325	3
2023 UNION PACIFIC ALCO A-A: 1950-51.				
Yellow with gray roof and nose.	2,000	2,800	4,500	8
Yellow with gray roof.	150	300	450	4
Silver with gray roof.	150	300	450	4
2024 CHESAPEAKE & OHIO ALCO A: 1969 only, unpainted dark blue body.	35	60	90	3
2025 2-6-2 STEAM: 1947-49, came with 2466WX or 6466WX tender.				
White "2025" stamped on boiler front.	85	125	200	5

2028 Pennsylvania GP-7

2031 Rock Island Alco A-A

2032 Erie Alco A-A

2033 Union Pacific Alco A-A

	VG	EX	LN	RARITY
Red keystone decal on boiler front.	70	100	175	2
2025 2-6-4 STEAM: 1952 only, with 6466W tender.	85	125	200	3
2026 2-6-2 STEAM: 1948-49, with 6466WX tender.				
Baldwin disc.	75	100	150	4
Spoke wheels.	50	75	100	2
2026 2-6-4 STEAM: 1951-53, with 6066T, 6466T or 6466W tender. Reduce listed values 1/3 for non-whistling tenders.				
Number rubber stamped in silver.	65	95	150	2
Number heat stamped in white.	90	125	185	3
2028 PENNSYLVANIA GP-7: 1955.				
Gold rubber-stamped lettering, gold frame.	250	425	650	6
Yellow rubber-stamped lettering, gold frame.	225	350	500	5
Tan frame.	350	600	925	8
2029 2-6-4 STEAM: 1964-69, Reduce listed values 1/3 for non-whistling tenders.				
With 1060T, 234T or 234W "Lionel Lines" tender.	55	75	125	4
With 234W "Pennsylvania" tender.	250	275	325	7
"Made in Japan."	65	100	150	5
2031 ROCK ISLAND ALCO A-A: 1952-54, painted black with broad red stripe.	250	375	575	6
2032 ERIE ALCO A-A: 1952-54, painted black with narrow yellow striping.	125	225	350	4
2033 UNION PACIFIC ALCO A-A: 1952-54, painted silver with silver roof.	150	275	450	3
2034 2-4-2 STEAM: 1952 only, came with a 6066T tender.	15	35	60	2
2035 2-6-4 STEAM: 1950-51, came with the 6466W tender.	75	125	200	3
2036 2-6-4 STEAM: 1950 only, with 6466W tender.	90	150	225	2

2037-50 2-6-4 Steam

2240 Wabash F-3 A-B

2242 New Haven F-3 A-B

2245 The Texas Special F-3 A-B

	VG	EX	LN	RARITY
2037 2-6-4 STEAM: 1953-55, 1957-63, came with 6026W, 233W or 234W whistle tender, or non-whistling 6066T, 6026T or 1130T tender. Reduce the values listed 1/3 for non-whistle tender.	75	120	175	2
2037-500 2-6-4 STEAM: 1957-58, pink, with 1130T-500 pink tender.	450	700	1,000	6
2041 ROCK ISLAND ALCO A-A: 1969, unpainted black plastic bodies with wide red stripe.	75	115	150	3
2046 4-6-4 STEAM: 1950-51, 1953, came with 2046W tender.				
Silver numbers with die-cast trailing truck.	140	200	275	3
White numbers with plastic and sheet metal trailing truck.	140	200	275	3
2055 4-6-4 STEAM: 1953-55, came with 6026W or 2046W tender.	140	200	275	3
2056 4-6-4 STEAM: 1952 only, came with 2046W tender.	175	250	350	3
2065 4-6-4 STEAM: 1954-56, came with 6026W or 2046W tender.	175	250	325	4
2240 WABASH F-3 A-B: 1956 only, molded in medium blue painted blue with the roof and upper body painted gray, the white band was silk-screened on. The final segment of the B-unit's white stripe, near "Built by Lionel" is one-half inch long.	475	750	1,200	4
2242 NEW HAVEN F-3 A-B: 1958-59, heat-stamped white "NH" on the nose door.	700	1,250	2,000	6
2243 SANTA FE F-3 A-B: 1955-57.				
High profile molded cab door ladder.	325	500	750	3
Flush molded cab door ladder.	275	450	675	3
2243C SANTA FE F-3 B-UNIT: 1955-57, not originally sold separately, but often sold individually on the collector market.	150	225	300	3
2245 THE TEXAS SPECIAL F-3 A-B: 1954-55, painted glossy red with white silk-screened lower panels. The red lettering on the sides of the units was actually the red paint that had been masked off. Horizontal motors in 1954, vertical in 1955.				
B-unit with open portholes.	400	600	900	5
Late 1955 B-unit with molded closed porthole.	750	1,000	1,500	7
2257 LIONEL-SP CABOOSE: 1947.				
Red or red-orange, no stack.	3	5	10	2

2321 Lackawanna FM

2329 Virginian EL-C Rectifier

2332 Pennsylvania GG1

2333 Santa Fe F-3 A-A

	VG	EX	LN	RARITY
Red-orange with matching stack.	100	225	400	6
Tuscan with matching stack.	300	500	775	8
2321 LACKAWANNA FM: 1954-56.				
Maroon roof.	550	800	1,250	6
Gray roof.	375	500	750	4
2322 VIRGINIAN FM: 1965-66.				
Unpainted blue plastic with painted-on yellow trim.	400	600	800	4
Both blue and yellow painted on.	500	750	950	6
2328 BURLINGTON GP-7: 1955-56, painted silver body, red frame.	300	450	750	4
2329 VIRGINIAN EL-C RECTIFIER: 1958-59, blue-painted body with yellow frame.	500	800	1,250	5
2330 PENNSYLVANIA GG1: 1950, painted green.	700	1,400	2,100	5
2331 VIRGINIAN FM: 1955-58.				
Molded gray body painted yellow and blue.	1,000	1,350	2,100	7
Molded gray body painted black and yellow.	850	1,200	1,750	6
Molded blue body with yellow painted on.	600	800	1,150	5
2332 PENNSYLVANIA GG1: 1947-49.				
Green.	250	450	750	3
Black.	600	1,000	2,000	8
2333 SANTA FE F-3 A-A: 1948-49.				
Clear, unpainted body.	3,000	5,000	7,000	8
Silver and red painted body.	300	600	1,200	4
2334 NEW YORK CENTRAL F-3 A-A: 1948-49.				
Rubber-stamped lettering.	350	650	1,300	5

2338 The Milwaukee Road with orange stripe on cab

2341 Jersey Central FM

2343 Santa Fe F-3 B-Unit

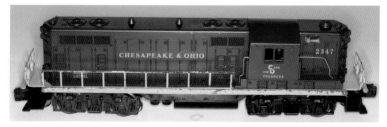

2347 Chesapeake & Ohio GP-7

	VG	EX	LN	RARITY
Heat-stamped lettering.	300	600	1,200	4
2337 WABASH GP-7: 1958, unpainted blue plastic body.	250	350	525	5
2338 THE MILWAUKEE ROAD GP-7: 1955-56.				
Translucent orange plastic body with orange stripe on cab.	900	1,500	2,250	6
Translucent orange plastic body with no cab stripe.	175	275	400	4
Opaque orange plastic bodies with no cab stripe.	175	275	400	3
2339 WABASH GP-7: 1957, unpainted blue plastic body.	200	300	450	5
2340 PENNSYLVANIA GG1: 1955.				
Painted green.	700	1,250	2,200	5
Painted Tuscan red.	900	1,500	2,550	6
2341 JERSEY CENTRAL FM: 1956 only, molded blue plastic body.				
Gloss orange.	1,400	2,350	3,500	7
Matte orange paint.	1,100	2,000	2,580	6
2343 SANTA FE F-3 A-A: 1950-52, painted red and silver.	300	500	1,200	3
2343C SANTA FE F-3 B-UNIT: 1950-55, screen-type (50-51) or molded louver roof vents.	150	250	450	4
2344 NEW YORK CENTRAL F-3 A-A: 1950-52.	350	600	1,100	3
2344C NEW YORK CENTRAL F-3 B-UNIT: 1950-55, screen-type (50-51) or molded louver roof vents.	175	300	450	4
2345 WESTERN PACIFIC F-3 A-A: 1952, painted silver and orange.	1,200	2,100	3,500	6
2346 BOSTON AND MAINE GP-9: 1965-66, black plastic body painted blue.	200	300	425	4
2347 CHESAPEAKE & OHIO GP-7: 1965 only, body painted blue with yellow heat-stamped markings.	1,500	2,500	3,700	8
2348 MINNEAPOLIS & ST LOUIS GP-9: 1958-59, painted red, and a white stripe painted on the middle of each side, the cab roof was painted blue, and red and white lettering was heat stamped on.	225	350	500	5

2350 New Haven EP-5

2354 New York Central F-3 A-A

2356 Southern F-3 A-A

2358 Great Northern EP-5

	VG	EX	LN	RARITY
2349 NORTHERN PACIFIC GP-9: 1959-60, painted black, brilliant gold-painted ends and side stripes.	275	450	650	6
2350 NEW HAVEN EP-5: 1956-58.				
Orange "N," a black "H," painted nose.	1,000	1,600	2,700	8
Orange "N," a black "H," decal nose.	700	1,200	1,800	7
White "N," orange "H," painted nose.	500	750	1,100	6
White "N," orange "H," decal nose.	225	400	550	3
2351 MILWAUKEE ROAD EP-5: 1957-58, yellow-painted body with a maroon-painted stripe in the middle and a black-painted upper quarter and roof, heat-stamped yellow lettering.	350	500	750	6
2352 PENNSYLVANIA EP-5: 1957-58, Tuscan-painted body.	350	500	750	5
2353 SANTA FE F-3 A-A: 1953-55, painted silver and red.	325	650	1,000	3
2354 NEW YORK CENTRAL F-3 A-A: 1953-55.	300	550	900	4
2355 WESTERN PACIFIC F-3 A-A: 1953, silver and orange paint.	900	1,800	3,000	7
2356 SOUTHERN F-3 A-A: 1954-56, green-painted body had its lower side panels and nose painted gray with rubber-stamped yellow stripes and lettering.	700	1,250	2,100	5
2356C SOUTHERN F-3 B-UNIT: 1954-56, decorated to match the 2356 A-A units.	250	400	550	6
2357 LIONEL-SP CABOOSE: 1947-48.				
Tuscan body and stack.	15	25	30	2
Tile red body, no stack.	65	125	225	5
Red body and stack.	250	450	750	8
2358 GREAT NORTHERN EP-5: 1959-60, "Great Northern" heat stamped on sides in yellow, end markings, number and "BLT BY LIONEL" were a large decal.	650	1,100	1,900	6
2359 BOSTON & MAINE GP-9: 1961-62, black plastic body painted blue, cab painted black, white heat-stamped lettering.	200	300	450	4
2360 PENNSYLVANIA GG1: 1956-58.				
Green with five stripes.	700	1,400	2,400	6

2360 Pennsylvania GG1

2363 Illinois Central F-3 A-B

2368 Baltimore & Ohio F-3 A-B

2378 Milwaukee Road F-3 A-B

	VG	EX	LN	RARITY
Tuscan with five stripes.	800	1,500	2,500	6
Tuscan with single stripe rubber stamped.	650	1,300	2,200	5
Tuscan with single stripe painted on.	650	1,100	1,750	6
Tuscan with single stripe decal.	650	1,100	1,750	6

2363 ILLINOIS CENTRAL F-3 A-B: 1955-56.

	VG	EX	LN	RARITY
Unpainted orange stripe.	400	800	1,500	6
Painted orange stripe.	400	800	1,500	5

2365 CHESAPEAKE & OHIO GP-7: 1962-63, painted blue with yellow heat-stamped markings.

	VG	EX	LN	RARITY
	200	325	475	4

2367 WABASH F-3 A-B: 1955 only, molded in royal blue plastic, A-unit painted, B-unit unpainted. The final segment of white stripe on B-unit, near the "Built by Lionel" marking is 1/8-inches long.

	VG	EX	LN	RARITY
Rubber-stamped B-unit lettering.	1,100	1,900	3,200	7
Heat-stamped B-unit lettering.	700	1,150	1,750	5

2368 BALTIMORE & OHIO F-3 A-B: 1956 only.

	VG	EX	LN	RARITY
Unpainted blue plastic.	1,600	2,400	3,600	6
Blue-painted gray plastic body.	2,000	2,800	4,150	7

2373 CANADIAN PACIFIC F-3 A-A: 1957, painted gray and brown with yellow heat-stamped stripes and lettering.

	VG	EX	LN	RARITY
	1,100	1,800	3,000	6

2378 MILWAUKEE ROAD F-3 A-B: 1956 only, unpainted gray bodies, painted-on red stripe and yellow heat-stamped delineating stripes. Each unit with or without a thin yellow roofline stripe, matched combinations are preferred.

	VG	EX	LN	RARITY
	1,400	2,400	3,400	6

2379 RIO GRANDE F-3 A-B: 1957-58, painted yellow, black horizontal stripes and side lettering were heat stamped.

	VG	EX	LN	RARITY
	1,000	1,600	2,500	5

2383 SANTA FE F-3 A-A: 1958-66, silver and red, or silver and orange-red.

	VG	EX	LN	RARITY
	275	450	700	3

2400 MAPLEWOOD PULLMAN: 1948-49, painted green with yellow stripes and window outlines, dark gray roof.

	VG	EX	LN	RARITY
	90	140	200	4

2401 HILLSIDE OBSERVATION: 1948-49, matches 2400.

	VG	EX	LN	RARITY
	85	125	175	4

2402 Chatham Pullman

2412 Santa Fe Vista Dome

2420 D. L. & W. Wrecking Car

2420 with light gray frame

	VG	EX	LN	RARITY
2402 CHATHAM PULLMAN: 1948-49, matches 2400.	90	140	200	4
2404 SANTA FE VISTA DOME: 1964-65, no lights or silhouetted window strips.	35	70	100	2
2405 SANTA FE PULLMAN: 1964-65, matches 2404.	35	70	100	2
2406 SANTA FE OBSERVATION: 1964-65, matches 2404.	30	60	90	2
2408 SANTA FE VISTA DOME: 1966 only, has lights and silhouetted window strips.	40	70	100	2
2409 SANTA FE PULLMAN: 1966 only, matches 2408.	40	70	100	2
2410 SANTA FE OBSERVATION: 1966 only, matches 2408.	35	60	90	2
2411 FLATCAR: 1946-48.				
Loaded with steel pipe with groove inside.	75	100	150	5
Loaded with 3/8-inch diameter wooden dowels.	20	30	42	3
2412 SANTA FE VISTA DOME: 1959-63, blue stripe, illuminated, with silhouetted window strips.	30	60	90	3
2414 SANTA FE PULLMAN: 1959-63, matches 2412.	30	60	90	3
2416 SANTA FE OBSERVATION: 1959-63, matches 2412.	25	55	80	3
2419 D. L. & W. WRECKING CAR: 1946-47.	20	35	50	3
2420 D. L. & W. WRECKING CAR: 1946-47, dark gray cab, die-cast frame.				
Dark gray heat-stamped lettering.	60	100	150	4
Light gray frame, rubber-stamped sans-serif lettering.	150	200	325	7
Light gray frame, heat-stamped serif lettering.	75	125	175	5
Dark gray frame, rubber-stamped sans-serif lettering.	125	175	275	6
2421 MAPLEWOOD PULLMAN: 1950-51.				
Gray roof.	60	90	125	3
1952-53, silver roof.	50	75	100	3
2422 CHATHAM PULLMAN: matches 2421.				
1950-51, gray roof.	60	90	125	3

2429 Livingston Pullman

2441 Observation

2442 Clifton Vista Dome

	VG	EX	LN	RARITY
1952-53, silver roof.	50	75	100	3
2423 HILLSIDE OBSERVATION: Matches 2421.				
1950-51, gray roof.	60	80	100	3
1952-53, silver roof.	50	70	90	3
2429 LIVINGSTON PULLMAN: 1952-53, matches 2421.	90	125	180	4
2430 PULLMAN: 1946-47, sheet metal with blue body with silver roof.	20	50	80	3
2431 OBSERVATION: 1946-47, matches 2430.	20	50	80	3
2432 CLIFTON VISTA DOME: 1954-58, silver, illuminated, with silhouetted window strips and red lettering.	25	50	75	2
2434 NEWARK PULLMAN: 1954-58, matches 2432.	25	50	75	2
2435 ELIZABETH PULLMAN: 1954-58, matches 2432.	40	75	125	4
2436 SUMMIT OBSERVATION: 1954-56, matches 2432.	35	60	100	2
2436 MOOSEHEART OBSERVATION: 1957-58, matches 2432.	35	60	100	2
2440 PULLMAN: 1946-47, two-tone green sheet metal silver rubber-stamped or white heat-stamped lettering.	25	50	75	3
2441 OBSERVATION: 1946-47, two-tone green sheet metal silver rubber-stamped or white heat-stamped lettering.	25	50	75	3
2442 PULLMAN: 1946-48, brown sheet metal; silver rubber-stamped or white heat-stamped lettering.	25	50	75	3
2442 CLIFTON VISTA DOME: 1956, red stripe illuminated with silhouetted window strips.	75	125	175	4
2443 OBSERVATION: 1946-48, brown sheet metal; silver rubber-stamped or white heat-stamped lettering.	25	50	80	3
2444 NEWARK PULLMAN: 1956, matches 2442.	75	125	175	4
2445 ELIZABETH PULLMAN: 1956, matches 2442.	100	175	225	5
2446 SUMMIT PULLMAN: 1956, matches 2442.	75	125	175	4
2452 PENNSYLVANIA GONDOLA: 1945-47.	12	20	40	2

X2454 Pennsylvania

2460 Bucyrus Erie Crane

2465 Sunoco Tanker

2481 Plainfield Pullman

	VG	EX	LN	RARITY
2452X PENNSYLVANIA GONDOLA: 1946-47.	10	15	20	2
X2454 BABY RUTH BOXCAR: 1946-47.	15	25	35	3
X2454 PENNSYLVANIA: 1946 only.				
Orange doors.	125	175	275	7
Brown doors.	80	150	250	6
2456 LEHIGH VALLEY HOPPER: 1948 only, black painted body.	15	25	35	4
2457 PENNSYLVANIA CABOOSE: 1945-47, "477618" on side, red or black window frames. Has illumination and glazed windows.				
Brown body.	60	100	150	5
Red body.	20	30	40	3
X2458 PENNSYLVANIA BOXCAR: 1946-48, brown 9-1/4-inch double-door automobile car.	20	45	65	3
2460 BUCYRUS ERIE CRANE: 1946-50.				
Gray cab.	125	200	300	5
Black cab.	50	80	100	3
2461 TRANSFORMER CAR: 1947-48.				
Red transformer load.	60	100	150	5
Black transformer load.	45	75	100	4
2465 SUNOCO TANKER: 1946-48.				
"SUNOCO" logo decal centered.	100	150	250	6
"SUNOCO" logo decal offset.	5	8	12	3
2472 PENNSYLVANIA CABOOSE: 1946-47, numbered "477618" on sides, red, no illumination or window glazing.	15	25	35	3
2481 PLAINFIELD PULLMAN: 1950, yellow, red markings, gray roof.	150	225	375	5
2482 WESTFIELD PULLMAN: 1950, matches 2481.	150	225	375	5
2483 LIVINGSTON OBSERVATION: 1950, matches 2481.	125	200	325	5

2521 Observation/President McKinley

2530 Lionel Lines/Railway Express Agency

2542 Pennsylvania/Betsy Ross Dome

2550 Baltimore & Ohio RDC-4

	VG	EX	LN	RARITY
2521 OBSERVATION/PRESIDENT McKINLEY: 1962-66, extruded aluminum.	75	110	150	3
2522 VISTA DOME/PRESIDENT HARRISON: 1962-66, matches 2521.	75	110	150	3
2523 PULLMAN/PRESIDENT GARFIELD: 1962-66, matches 2521.	75	110	150	3
2530 LIONEL LINES/RAILWAY EXPRESS AGENCY: 1954-60, extruded aluminum baggage car.				
Large doors.	250	400	550	6
Small doors.	75	125	175	4
2531 LIONEL LINES/SILVER DAWN OBSERVATION: 1952-60, extruded aluminum.				
With fluted channels above and below the windows.	60	100	125	3
With flat channels above and below the windows.	125	160	200	6
2532 LIONEL LINES/SILVER RANGE DOME: 1952-60, matches 2531.				
With fluted channels above and below the windows.	60	100	125	3
With flat channels above and below the windows.	125	160	200	6
2533 LIONEL LINES/SILVER CLOUD PULLMAN: 1952-60, matches 2531.				
With fluted channels above and below the windows.	60	100	125	3
With flat channels above and below the windows.	125	160	200	6
2534 LIONEL LINES/SILVER BLUFF PULLMAN: 1952-60, matches 2531.				
With fluted channels above and below the windows.	60	100	125	3
With flat channels above and below the windows.	125	160	200	6
2541 PENNSYLVANIA/ALEXANDER HAMILTON OBSERVATION: 1955-56, extruded aluminum Congressional.	125	200	275	5
2542 PENNSYLVANIA/BETSY ROSS DOME: 1955-56, matches 2541.	125	200	275	5
2543 PENNSYLVANIA/WILLIAM PENN PULLMAN: 1955-56, matches 2541.	125	200	275	5
2544 PENNSYLVANIA/MOLLY PITCHER PULLMAN: 1955-56, matches 2541.	125	200	275	5
2550 BALTIMORE & OHIO RDC-4: 1957-58.	350	550	750	6

2553 Canadian Pacific/Blair Manor Pullman

2555 Sunoco Tanker

2561 Santa Fe/Vista Valley Pullman

2625 Irvington Pullman

	VG	EX	LN	RARITY
2551 CANADIAN PACIFIC/BANFF PARK OBSERVATION: 1957, extruded aluminum.	150	225	325	5
2552 CANADIAN PACIFIC/SKYLINE 500 DOME: 1957, matches 2551.	150	250	325	5
2553 CANADIAN PACIFIC/BLAIR MANOR PULLMAN: 1957, matches 2551.	225	350	500	6
2554 CANADIAN PACIFIC/CRAIG MANOR PULLMAN: 1957, matches 2551.	225	350	500	6
2555 SUNOCO TANKER: 1946-48.				
With "GAS" and "OILS" in SUNOCO logo, "2555" on side.	30	45	60	4
Without "GAS" and "OILS" in SUNOCO logo, "2555" on side.	30	45	60	4
With "GAS" and "OILS" in SUNOCO logo, "2555" on bottom.	20	40	55	3
Without "GAS" and "OILS" in SUNOCO logo, "2555" on bottom.	20	40	55	3
2559 BALTIMORE & OHIO RDC-9: 1957-58, nonpowered.	200	300	425	5
2560 LIONEL LINES CRANE: 1946-47, similar to prewar 2660 crane, green, brown or black two-piece boom.	45	65	125	4
2561 SANTA FE/VISTA VALLEY PULLMAN: 1959-61, extruded aluminum.	175	225	325	5
2562 SANTA FE/REGAL PASS DOME: 1959-61, matches 2561.	200	250	375	5
2563 SANTA FE/INDIAN FALLS PULLMAN: 1959-61, matches 2561.	200	250	375	5
2625 IRVINGTON PULLMAN: 1946-50.				
Plain windows.	125	225	350	3
Silhouetted windows (1950 only).	150	275	475	4
2625 MADISON PULLMAN: 1947, plain windows.	175	300	500	4
2625 MANHATTAN PULLMAN: 1947, plain windows.	175	300	500	4
2627 MADISON PULLMAN: 1948-50.				
Plain windows.	125	225	350	3
Silhouetted windows (1950 only).	150	275	475	4

2855 Sunoco Tanker

3330 Flatcar with Operating Submarine Kit

3356 Santa Fe Horse Car with Corral

	VG	EX	LN	RARITY
2628 MANHATTAN PULLMAN: 1948-50.				
Plain windows.	125	225	350	3
Silhouetted windows (1950 only).	150	275	400	4
2755 SUNOCO TANKER: 1945 only, silver.	70	100	185	5
X2758 PENNSYLVANIA BOXCAR: 1945-46, brown 9-1/4-inch double-door automobile car.	25	50	75	4
2855 SUNOCO TANKER: 1946-47.				
Black "GAS" and "OILS" in SUNOCO logo.	125	225	375	6
Black without "GAS" and "OILS" in SUNOCO logo.	125	225	375	6
Gray without "GAS" and "OILS" in SUNOCO logo.	80	175	225	5
3309 TURBO MISSILE LAUNCHING CAR: 1962-64, non-operating couplers.				
Light red.	20	35	55	3
Cherry red.	45	70	100	5
3330 FLATCAR WITH OPERATING SUBMARINE KIT: 1960-62, submarines lettered 3830, those lettered 3330 are forgeries.	100	150	225	5
3349 TURBO MISSILE FIRING CAR: 1962-65, unpainted red plastic, two operating couplers.	30	50	65	4
3349-100 TURBO MISSILE LAUNCHING CAR: 1963-64, one operating coupler.				
Red.	20	35	55	3
Olive drab.	200	350	500	7
3356 SANTA FE HORSE CAR WITH CORRAL: Reduce value by 50 percent if corral is missing.				
1956-60, bar-end metal.	100	140	180	4
1964-66, AAR-plastic trucks.	125	175	250	5
3357 HYDRAULIC PLATFORM MAINTENANCE CAR: 1962-64, with overhead "bridge," trip and police and hobo figures.	35	65	100	4
3359 LIONEL LINES DUMP CAR: 1955-58.	40	60	80	3

3360 Burro Crane

3366 Circus Car

3376 Bronx Zoo

3410 Helicopter
Launching Car

	VG	EX	LN	RARITY
3360 BURRO CRANE: 1956-57, with actuator, yellow.				
Painted.	425	650	900	6
Unpainted.	175	275	400	4
3361 LOG DUMP CAR: 1955-59, serif or sans-serif lettering, "336155" either to right or left of "LIONEL LINES."	25	35	55	4
3362 HELIUM TANK UNLOADING CAR: 1961-63, unpainted dark green plastic, white rubber-stamped "LIONEL LINES 3362," three "helium tanks" AAR trucks with operating couplers.	15	20	45	3
3362/3364 OPERATING UNLOADING CAR: 1969, unpainted dark green plastic, no markings, two "helium tanks," non-operating couplers.	15	35	75	6
3364 OPERATING LOG UNLOADING CAR: 1965-66, 1968, identical to the 3362, and rubber stamped "3362," came 3-5/8 x 6-inch wooden dowels stained brown.	15	30	70	5
3366 CIRCUS CAR: 1959-61, unpainted white body and doors, red-painted roofwalk. Reduce value 50 percent if matching corral and nine white horses are missing.	150	250	375	6
3370 WELLS FARGO SHERIFF & OUTLAW: 1961-64, action simulates gunfight.	25	50	90	5
3376 BRONX ZOO: 1960-66, 1969, blue car body. Giraffe "ducks" to avoid obstacle. Includes telltale and operating plate assembly.				
White lettering.	40	65	90	3
Yellow (1969) lettering.	175	300	450	8
3376-160 BRONX ZOO: Green body with yellow lettering.	85	110	150	5
3386 BRONX ZOO: 1960 only, blue with white markings, arch-bar trucks and non-operating couplers.	60	80	115	4
3409 OPERATING HELICOPTER LAUNCHING CAR: 1960-62, came with an operating single rotor helicopter with a gray body heat-stamped "NAVY."	100	165	275	6
3410 HELICOPTER LAUNCHING CAR: 1961-63, and carried a gray-bodied single rotor helicopter with heat-stamped "NAVY" with separate pale yellow tail rotor or solid yellow helicopter with integral tail.	60	100	150	5

3413 Mercury
Capsule
Launching Car

3429 U.S.M.C.
Operating
Helicopter
Launching Car

3435 Aquarium
Car

3444 Erie
Operating
Gondola

	VG	EX	LN	RARITY
3413 MERCURY CAPSULE LAUNCHING CAR: 1962-64, unpainted red plastic chassis with gray plastic superstructure. Came with parachute-equipped rocket.	100	160	250	6
3413-150 MERCURY CAPSULE LAUNCHING CAR: 1963, equipped with one operating and one non-operating coupler.	100	160	250	6

3419 OPERATING HELICOPTER LAUNCHING CAR: 1959-65, its body was made of blue plastic, which ranged from medium blue to a dark, almost purple shade. In 1959 the launch spindle was two inches in diameter, in subsequent years a 1-3/8-inch spindle was used, black or plated operating mechanism, single- or two-blade.

	VG	EX	LN	RARITY
Gray "Navy" helicopter.	50	90	175	3
All-yellow helicopter.	75	120	200	3
3424 WABASH BOXCAR WITH BRAKEMAN: 1956-58, with two contactor/pole-support assemblies and two telltale poles. The brakeman figures came in two colors; blue and white, and the car bodies came molded in both medium and dark blue, but there is no difference in value associated with either variation.	50	75	125	4
3428 UNITED STATES MAIL OPERATING BOXCAR: 1959-60, red, white and blue boxcar. Rubber figure of a blue or gray mailman ejects rubber "bag" of mail.	50	85	125	4

3429 U.S.M.C. OPERATING HELICOPTER LAUNCHING CAR: 1960, painted olive drab and white heat stamped "BUILT BY/LIONEL U. S. M. C. 3429."

	VG	EX	LN	RARITY
Came with single rotor operating helicopter with a gray body heat stamped "USMC" on the tail boom.	350	425	700	7

3434 OPERATING POULTRY DISPATCH: Man "sweeps" illuminated car with color chicken silhouettes.

	VG	EX	LN	RARITY
1959-60: bar-end metal trucks.	75	110	175	5
1964-66: AAR plastic trucks.	65	100	150	4

3435 AQUARIUM CAR: 1959-62, "fish," printed on film, "swim" in illuminated tank.

	VG	EX	LN	RARITY
Gold circle around "L" logo, gold "TANK No. 1" and "TANK No. 2" markings.	650	1,100	1,750	8
Gold "TANK No. 1" and "TANK No. 2" markings, no circle.	550	875	1,350	7
Gold markings without "TANK No. 1" and "TANK No. 2" or circle.	200	275	425	6
Yellow markings.	125	200	275	5
3444 ERIE OPERATING GONDOLA: 1957-1959.	50	75	110	3

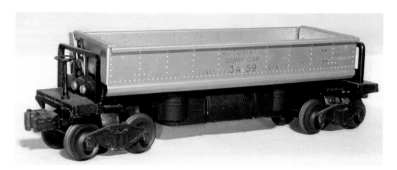

3459 Lionel Lines Dump Car

3461 Operating Lumber Car

X3464 NYC Boxcar

	VG	EX	LN	RARITY
3451 OPERATING LUMBER CAR: 1946-48, with five unstained 7/16 x 4-5/8-inch wooden dowels.	30	40	60	5
3454 AUTOMATIC MERCHANDISE BOXCAR: 1946-47, painted silver.				
Blue lettering.	75	110	175	4
Red lettering.	600	1,000	1,700	7
3456 N & W HOPPER: 1950-55, operating doors.	20	45	65	3
3459 LIONEL LINES DUMP CAR: 1946-48.				
Aluminum-colored dump bin.	150	225	450	6
Green dump bin.	40	80	110	4
Black dump bin.	25	50	80	3
3460 FLATCAR WITH TRAILERS: 1955-1957, unpainted green plastic trailers with removable roofs, die-cast landing gear and metal side signs reading "LIONEL TRAINS."	40	70	100	4
3461 OPERATING LUMBER CAR: 1949-55.				
Black frame.	20	35	50	3
Green frame.	25	55	90	4
3462 AUTOMATIC REFRIGERATED MILK CAR: 1947-48, if platform and milk cans are absent, the values should be reduced by 50 percent.				
Gloss cream.	75	125	200	7
Matte cream.	35	50	70	5
White painted body.	30	45	60	2
X3464 A. T. & S. F. BOXCAR: 1949-52, 9-1/4 inches long.				
Orange body.	12	20	30	2
Tan body.	275	400	650	7
X3464 NYC BOXCAR: 1949-52, 9-1/4 inches, tan.	12	20	30	2
3469 LIONEL LINES DUMP CAR: 1949-55, black.	30	40	60	3

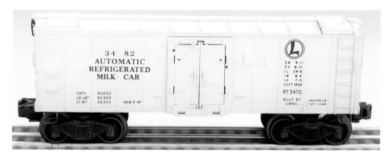

3482 Automatic Refrigerated Milk Car

3485-25 A. T. & S. F. Operating Boxcar

3494-550 Monon Operating Boxcar

3494-625 Soo Line Operating Boxcar

	VG	EX	LN	RARITY
3470 AERIAL TARGET LAUNCHING CAR: 1962-64, dark blue flatcar.	50	75	100	4
3470-100 AERIAL TARGET LAUNCHING CAR: 1963, powder blue.	200	325	475	7
3472 AUTOMATIC REFRIGERATED MILK CAR: 1949-53, painted cream or unpainted white with aluminum doors, or unpainted white with plastic doors. If platform and milk cans are absent, the values should be reduced by 50 percent.	30	45	60	2
3474 WESTERN PACIFIC BOXCAR: 1952-53, silver 9-1/4 inches long.	30	55	80	5
3482 AUTOMATIC REFRIGERATED MILK CAR: 1954-55, 9-1/4-inch long unpainted white milk car. Stamped "RT3472" or "RT3482" to right of door. If platform and milk cans are absent, the values should be reduced by 50 percent.				
Stamped "RT3472."	75	100	150	6
Stamped "RT3482."	40	60	85	5
3484 PENNSYLVANIA OPERATING BOXCAR: 1953, 10-5/8 inches long.	30	50	80	3
3484-25 A. T. & S. F. OPERATING BOXCAR: 1954, 1956, orange 10-5/8-inch long boxcar.				
Black lettering.	900	1,400	2,500	8
White lettering.	50	80	125	4
3494-1 PACEMAKER OPERATING BOXCAR: 1955, 10-5/8 inches long.	75	110	165	4
3494-150 MISSOURI PACIFIC LINES OPERATING BOXCAR: 1956, 10-5/8-inch long.	60	100	160	5
3494-275 STATE OF MAINE OPERATING BOXCAR: 1956-58, 10-5/8 inches long.				
With "3494275" stamped to the left of the door.	60	80	125	4
Without "3494275" stamped to the left of the door.	100	175	275	6
3494-550 MONON OPERATING BOXCAR: 1957-58, 10-5/8 inches long.	200	325	550	7
3494-625 SOO LINE OPERATING BOXCAR: 1957-58, 10-5/8 inches long.	200	325	575	7
3509 SATELLITE LAUNCHING CAR: 1961, unpainted dark green, gray and yellow.	40	65	100	5
3510 SATELLITE LAUNCHING CAR: 1962, bright red no number on car.	100	150	250	6

3530 Electro Mobile Power Generator Car

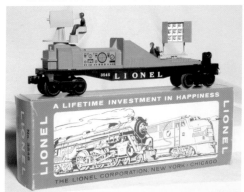

3545 Operating TV Monitor Car

3562-25 A. T. & S. F. Operating Barrel Car

3562-50 A. T. & S. F. Operating Barrel Car

	VG	EX	LN	RARITY
3512 OPERATING FIREMAN AND LADDER CAR: 1959-61.				
Black extension ladder.	75	125	180	5
Silver extension ladder.	100	160	250	7
3519 OPERATING SATELLITE LAUNCHING CAR: 1961-64, dark green unpainted plastic.	35	55	80	4
3520 LIONEL LINES SEARCHLIGHT CAR: 1952-53.				
Serif lettering.	75	125	180	6
Sans-serif lettering.	30	55	75	4
3530 ELECTRO MOBILE POWER GENERATOR CAR: 1956-58, white stripe stops at ladder or extends through the molded-in ladder on the right-hand end of the car.	50	100	150	5
3535 OPERATING SECURITY CAR WITH ROTATING SEARCHLIGHT: 1960-61.	75	115	175	4
3540 OPERATING RADAR CAR: 1959-62.	100	175	250	5
3545 OPERATING TV MONITOR CAR: 1961-62.	125	200	300	5
3559 COAL DUMP: 1946-48, black or brown Bakelite mechanism housing.	20	35	50	3
3562-1 A. T. & S. F. OPERATING BARREL CAR: 1954.				
Black with black trough.	110	175	250	4
Black with yellow trough.	110	175	200	4
Gray with red lettering.	1,000	1,500	2,300	8
3562-25 A. T. & S. F. OPERATING BARREL CAR: 1954 only, gray painted body marked "356225" on car side.				
Red heat-stamped markings.	250	400	650	6
Gray painted body with blue markings.	40	65	85	3
Yellow painted body with black heat-stamped markings.	1,200	1,800	2,900	8
3562-50 A. T. & S. F. OPERATING BARREL CAR: 1955-56, marked "356250" on car side.				
Yellow painted body.	60	95	150	4
Yellow unpainted body.	40	70	85	3

3619 Helicopter
Reconnaissance Car

3650 Lionel Lines
Searchlight Extension Car

3656 Lionel Lines
Operating Cattle Car

3662 Automatic
Refrigerated Milk Car

	VG	EX	LN	RARITY
3562-75 A. T. & S. F. OPERATING BARREL CAR: Orange unpainted body marked "356275."	55	90	150	4
3619 HELICOPTER RECONNAISSANCE CAR: 1962-64, it had an unpainted yellow body, red HO-Gauge helicopter.				
Light yellow plastic.	60	100	150	4
Dark yellow plastic.	100	175	275	6
3620 LIONEL LINES SEARCHLIGHT CAR: 1954-56.				
Searchlight housing made of unpainted gray plastic.	30	40	60	4
Searchlight housing made of unpainted orange plastic.	100	140	200	7
Searchlight housing made of orange plastic painted gray.	125	175	250	7
Searchlight housing made of gray plastic painted gray.	30	40	60	4
3650 LIONEL LINES SEARCHLIGHT EXTENSION CAR: 1956-59, values include die-cast spool handle.				
Light-gray frame.	40	60	80	4
Dark-gray frame.	80	120	175	6
Olive-gray frame.	125	175	275	7
3656 LIONEL LINES OPERATING CATTLE CAR: 1949-55, reduce value 50 percent if matching corral and cattle are missing.				
Heat-stamped black lettering, adhesive "Armour" logo.	150	225	300	7
Heat-stamped white lettering, adhesive "Armour" logo.	60	90	125	6
Heat-stamped white lettering, no "Armour" logo.	50	75	110	4
3662 AUTOMATIC REFRIGERATED MILK CAR: 1955-60 and 1964-66, if platform and milk cans are absent, the values should be reduced by 50 percent.				
Painted white, heat stamped "NEW 4-55."	50	75	115	5
Unpainted white, heat stamped "NEW 4-55."	45	70	100	4
AAR trucks, unpainted white, heat stamped "NEW 4-55."	50	75	115	5
1964-66, unpainted white, AAR-type trucks, no "NEW 4-55."	40	70	100	4

3666 Minuteman

3672 Corn Products
Co. - Bosco

3854 Automatic
Merchandise Car

X4454 Baby
Ruth Boxcar

	VG	EX	LN	RARITY

3665 MINUTEMAN: 1961-64, unpainted white body with red and white rocket with blue rubber nose cone.

	VG	EX	LN	RARITY
Dark blue, almost purple roof.	60	90	125	4
Light-blue roof.	150	200	350	7

3666 MINUTEMAN: unpainted white body, housing large olive drab cannon with four wooden artillery shells.

	350	550	850	8

3672 CORN PRODUCTS CO.-BOSCO: 1959-60, if platform and milk cans are absent, the values should be reduced by 50 percent.

	VG	EX	LN	RARITY
Unpainted yellow body.	225	350	525	6
Painted yellow.	250	375	575	6

3820 U.S.M.C. OPERATING SUBMARINE CAR: 1960-62, painted olive drab body carrying factory-assembled gray "U.S. NAVY 3830" submarine. Be aware that in addition to reproduction 3830 submarines, forgeries stamped "U.S.M.C. 3820" also exist.

	120	225	350	6

3830 SUBMARINE CAR: 1960-63, unpainted blue carrying submarine lettered "U.S. NAVY 3830."

	90	115	150	4

3854 AUTOMATIC MERCHANDISE CAR: 1946-47, Bakelite body painted brown, with six plastic "crates" (actually cubes) engraved "BABY RUTH." Cubes came in black, brown and red, with brown being the most common.

	700	1,000	1,600	8

3927 TRACK CLEANING CAR: 1956-60.

	40	65	90	2

4357 LIONEL-SP CABOOSE: 1948-49, Tuscan-painted plastic body.

	VG	EX	LN	RARITY
Plastic smokejack painted body color.	85	150	250	5
Die-cast smokejack finished in black.	90	165	265	5

4452 PENNSYLVANIA GONDOLA: 1946-49.

	75	115	150	4

X4454 BABY RUTH BOXCAR: 1946-49.

	90	175	300	6

4457 PENNSYLVANIA CABOOSE: 1946-47, steel-bodied caboose painted red.

	75	150	250	6

5459 LIONEL LINES DUMP CAR: 1946-49.

	100	175	275	4

6002 NEW YORK CENTRAL GONDOLA: 1950 only. It was not supplied with a load.

	12	20	30	4

6014 Airex Boxcar

6014 Chun King Boxcar

6014 Frisco Boxcar

6014 Wix Filters Boxcar

	VG	EX	LN	RARITY
X6004 BABY RUTH BOXCAR: 1950 only, unpainted orange.	5	7	10	2
6007 LIONEL LINES CABOOSE: 1950 only, unpainted red plastic.	5	10	15	2
6012 LIONEL GONDOLA: 1951-56, unpainted black plastic body.	5	8	15	1
6014 AIREX BOXCAR: 1959 only.	35	50	75	5
X6014 BABY RUTH BOXCAR: 1951-56, these cars had metal trucks.				
Red body with white lettering.	7	12	16	2
Flat white body and black lettering.	4	8	10	1
Glossy white body with black lettering.	4	8	10	1
6014 BOSCO BOXCAR: 1958, AAR-type trucks.				
Unpainted red body.	6	9	12	1
Unpainted white body.	30	50	75	6
Unpainted orange body.	6	9	12	1
6014 CHUN KING BOXCAR: 1956.	100	150	275	7
6014 FRISCO BOXCAR: 1957, 1963–69.				
1957, unpainted red body.	4	6	10	1
1957, flat white version.	4	6	10	1
1957, orange.	35	60	80	6
1963, lighter white.	4	6	10	1
With coin slot in the roof.	50	75	125	7
1969, very glossy white.	4	6	10	2
1969, orange.	20	30	45	4
6014 WIX FILTERS BOXCAR: 1959 only.				
Cream color unpainted body.	100	150	275	7

6015 Sunoco
Tanker

6017 Lionel
Caboose

6017-50 United
States Marine
Corps Caboose

6017 Boston &
Marine Caboose

	VG	EX	LN	RARITY
Snow white unpainted body.	120	180	300	6
6015 SUNOCO TANKER: 1954-55.				
Painted yellow.	60	100	150	5
Molded medium-yellow.	5	8	10	1
Molded dark-yellow body.	5	8	10	2
6017 LIONEL LINES CABOOSE: 1951-62.				
Unpainted red body, metal trucks.	5	10	15	2
Unpainted Tuscan body supplanted the red previously used. These cars had bar-end trucks and a single magnetic coupler.	4	7	10	1
Semi-gloss Tuscan paint.	50	75	100	6
Distinctly glossy Tuscan red.	75	125	200	7
Painted maroon.	8	12	16	3
Painted tile red.	6	9	12	2
Painted brown.	2	4	6	1
6017 LIONEL CABOOSE: 1956 only, often mistaken for the common 6017 Lionel Lines.	35	60	90	5
6017-50 UNITED STATES MARINE CORPS CABOOSE: 1958 only, dark blue.	35	60	90	4
6017 LIONEL LINES CABOOSE: 1958 only, painted light gray.	15	30	45	3
6017 BOSTON & MAINE CABOOSE: 1959, 1962 and 1965-66.				
Painted medium-blue.	20	35	60	4
Semi-gloss medium-blue bodies.	15	30	50	3
Semi-gloss light blue.	15	30	50	3
Painted dark blue; almost purple.	275	425	650	6
6017 A. T. & S. F. CABOOSE: 1959-60, painted light gray.	20	30	45	4

6024 RCA
Whirlpool
Boxcar

6025 Gulf
Tank Car

6027
Alaska
Railroad
Caboose

6037 Lionel
Lines
Caboose

	VG	EX	LN	RARITY
6017-200 UNITED STATES NAVY CABOOSE: 1960 only.	50	75	110	5
6017-235 A. T. & S. F. CABOOSE: 1962 only, painted red.	30	50	75	4
6024 RCA WHIRLPOOL BOXCAR: 1957 only.	35	60	80	5
6024 SHREDDED WHEAT BOXCAR: 1957 only.	12	20	30	3
6025 GULF TANK CAR: 1956-58, unpainted black plastic body with white rubber-stamped lettering.	5	10	15	2
Painted-black body with white rubber-stamped lettering.	5	10	15	3
Unpainted gray body with blue heat-stamped lettering.	5	10	15	3
Orange body with blue lettering.	16	25	40	4
6027 ALASKA RAILROAD CABOOSE: 1959 only, painted dark-blue, heat stamped in yellow.	40	65	100	5
6032 LIONEL GONDOLA: 1952-54, unpainted black plastic.	5	8	15	2
X6034 BABY RUTH BOXCAR: 1953-54, unpainted orange.	7	10	15	1
6035 SUNOCO TANK CAR: 1952-53, unpainted gray body.	3	8	15	1
6037 LIONEL LINES CABOOSE: 1952-54.				
Unpainted Tuscan bodies.	3	5	7	1
Unpainted red bodies with white heat-stamped markings.	25	40	70	4
6042 LIONEL GONDOLA: 1959-64, equipped with arch-bar or AAR trucks, with or without operating couplers.				
Black.	5	8	12	2
Blue.	5	8	12	2
Blue, unmarked.	10	15	18	2
6044 AIREX BOXCAR: 1959-61, white and yellow heat-stamped lettering.				
Medium blue.	10	18	25	3
Teal blue body.	55	85	125	6

6044 Airex Boxcar

6044-1X McCall's - Nestle's Boxcar

6045 Cities Service Tank Car

6050 Libby's Tomato Juice Boxcar

	VG	EX	LN	RARITY
Very dark blue, approaching purple.	175	275	425	8
6044-1X McCALL'S-NESTLE'S BOXCAR: Produced in the early 1960s, unpainted blue body was decorated by pasting a miniature McCall's-Nestlé's billboard on each side.	700	1,000	1,900	8
6045 LIONEL LINES TANK CAR: 1959-64.				
Unpainted gray.	15	30	45	3
Unpainted beige.	15	30	45	3
Unpainted orange.	20	50	75	4
6045 CITIES SERVICE TANK CAR: 1960-61, green.	20	50	75	4
6047 LIONEL LINES CABOOSE: 1959-62.				
Unpainted medium red.	3	5	10	2
Unpainted coral pink.	20	40	65	5
6050 LIBBY'S TOMATO JUICE BOXCAR: 1963, unpainted white body with red and blue lettering and a red, blue and green tomato juice logo.	20	35	60	4
6050 LIONEL SAVINGS BANK BOXCAR: 1961.				
"BUILT BY LIONEL" abbreviated as "BLT."	20	30	45	4
"BUILT BY LIONEL" spelled out.	50	75	100	6
6050 SWIFT BOXCAR: 1962-63, unpainted red with white heat-stamped lettering.	12	20	30	3
With two holes in the roofwalk, a leftover from 3357.	30	50	90	6
6057 LIONEL LINES CABOOSE: 1959-62, 1969.				
Painted red.	35	60	90	6
Unpainted red.	6	10	15	2
Coral-pink bodies.	25	45	65	4
6057-50 LIONEL LINES CABOOSE: 1962, unpainted orange.	15	25	40	3

6058 Chesapeake & Ohio Caboose

6059 M & St. L Caboose

6110 2-4-2 Steam

6111/6121 Flatcar

	VG	EX	LN	RARITY
6058 CHESAPEAKE & OHIO CABOOSE: 1961, painted dark yellow.	20	35	60	5
6059 M & St. L CABOOSE: 1961-69.				
Painted red.	15	20	30	5
Unpainted red.	4	8	12	3
Unpainted maroon.	8	10	16	4
6059-50 M & St. L: 1963-64, unpainted red body with white heat-stamped markings.	12	18	25	5
6062 NEW YORK CENTRAL GONDOLA: 1959-1962, 1969.				
Black with metal underframe.	25	40	60	5
Unpainted black, no metal underframe.	15	20	28	2
Painted black.	15	20	28	2
6067 CABOOSE: 1961-62, unlettered.				
Red unpainted plastic.	2	4	7	1
Yellow plastic.	12	20	35	3
Brown plastic.	20	35	50	4
6076 A. T. & S. F. HOPPER: Unpainted gray, black heat-stamped lettering.	15	30	40	4
6076 LEHIGH VALLEY HOPPER: 1961-65.				
Light-red body.	10	14	18	2
Dark-red body.	10	14	18	2
Black body.	10	14	18	2
Gray body.	10	14	18	2
Pale-yellow-painted body.	400	800	1,800	8
6110 2-4-2 STEAM: 1950 only, with a 6001T tender.	25	40	55	2
6111/6121 FLATCAR: 1955-58, fire engine red with white lettering.	10	15	20	3

6119-25 D. L. & W. Work Caboose

6119-50 D. L. & W. Work Caboose

6119-75 D. L. & W. Work Caboose

6119-125 Rescue Caboose

	VG	EX	LN	RARITY
Bright red with white lettering.	10	15	20	3
Maroon with white lettering.	30	50	80	7
Medium lemon yellow with black lettering.	10	15	20	3
Medium lemon yellow with white lettering.	200	350	500	8
Light gray with white lettering.	10	15	20	3
Glossy dark gunmetal gray with white lettering.	10	15	20	3
Gray-drab with white lettering.	10	15	20	3
Dark gray with white lettering.	10	15	20	3
Battleship gray with white lettering.	10	15	20	3
6112 LIONEL GONDOLA: 1956-58.				
Black body with white lettering.	5	8	12	1
Blue body with white lettering.	10	14	18	2
White body with black lettering.	15	30	50	4
6119 D. L. & W. WORK CABOOSE: 1955-56, unpainted red open tool compartment and unpainted red plastic cab.	12	25	40	3
6119-25 D. L. & W. WORK CABOOSE: 1956 only, overall orange work caboose.	20	35	55	4
6119-50 D. L. & W. WORK CABOOSE: 1956 only, all-brown 6119.	25	45	75	5
6119-75 D. L. & W. WORK CABOOSE: 1957, an unpainted gray tool compartment and cab, black heat-stamped sans-serif lettering.	12	25	45	4
Closely spaced, black rubber-stamped-serif lettering on its frame.	125	225	375	8
6119-100 D. L. & W. WORK CABOOSE: 1957-66, unpainted gray tool compartment and an unpainted red cab.	8	15	25	2
Cab painted red.	50	100	150	6
With builder's plate heat stamped "BUILT BY/LIONEL."	75	125	175	6
6119-125 RESCUE CABOOSE: 1964 only, cab and tool compartment unpainted olive drab plastic.	100	175	275	6

6151 Flatcar with Range Patrol Truck

6162 New York Central Gondola

6162-60 Alaska Railroad Gondola

6167 Undecorated Caboose

	VG	EX	LN	RARITY
6120 UNDECORATED CABOOSE: Unpainted yellow tool compartment and cab.	20	30	45	3
6130 A. T. & S. F. CABOOSE: 1961-65, 1969.				
Red tool compartment and a red cab.	15	25	40	4
1966 with additional, but unused letterboard.	90	150	250	7
6142 LIONEL GONDOLA: 1963-66, 1969.				
Black body.	5	8	12	1
Unlettered green body.	10	12	15	2
Unlettered bright translucent green body.	30	40	50	4
Blue body stamped "Lionel" and "6142."	5	8	10	1
Green body stamped "Lionel" and "6142."	5	8	10	1
Undecorated olive drab body; listed as 6142-75 in the Lionel Service Manual.	75	110	165	5
6151 FLATCAR WITH RANGE PATROL TRUCK: 1958 only, white cabbed-black bodied truck made by Pyro heat stamped "LIONEL RANCH."	65	110	160	5
6162 NEW YORK CENTRAL GONDOLA: 1959-68, commonly with a load of three white canisters, blue body with "NEW 2-49" markings on car sides.	10	12	15	1
Teal body with "NEW 2-49" markings on car sides.	10	12	15	1
Blue without "NEW 2-49" markings.	10	12	15	1
Red, without "NEW 2-49" markings.	85	125	200	6
6162-60 ALASKA RAILROAD GONDOLA: 1959, unpainted yellow plastic with dark-blue with heat-stamped markings.	40	55	80	4
6167 LIONEL LINES CABOOSE: 1963-64.				
Unpainted red.	4	7	10	1
Painted red.	60	100	175	6
6167 UNDECORATED CABOOSE: Unpainted olive-drab.	200	375	600	7

6167-85 Union Pacific Caboose

6219 C & O Work Caboose

6220 A. T. & S. F. NW-2

6250 Seaboard NW-2

	VG	EX	LN	RARITY
6167-25 UNDECORATED CABOOSE: 1963-64, red.	5	7	10	1
6167-50 UNDECORATED CABOOSE: unpainted yellow body.	10	20	35	4
6167-85 UNION PACIFIC CABOOSE: 1963-66, 1969, unpainted yellow body, black heat-stamped markings.	10	16	25	3
6167-100 LIONEL LINES CABOOSE: 1963-64, unpainted red body.	5	10	14	2
6167-125 UNDECORATED CABOOSE: 1963-64, unpainted red body.	5	7	10	1
6167-150 LIONEL LINES CABOOSE: 1963-64, unpainted red body.	5	10	14	2
6167-1967 T. T. O. S. HOPPER (Toy Train Operating Society): 1967, unpainted olive with metallic gold heat-stamped lettering.	45	65	100	6
6175 ROCKET FLATCAR: 1958-61, white plastic rocket load heat stamped "BUILT BY/ LIONEL" and "U S NAVY" in blue.				
Unpainted red plastic.	35	60	85	4
Unpainted black plastic.	35	60	85	4
6176 LEHIGH VALLEY HOPPER: 1964-66, 1969.				
Bright yellow.	12	18	25	2
Dark yellow.	8	10	16	1
Gray.	8	10	16	1
Black.	10	15	20	2
6219 C & O WORK CABOOSE: 1960, tool compartment and cab painted dark blue.	30	50	75	5
6220 A. T. & S. F. NW-2: 1949-50, black, die-cast frame.				
With "6220" stamped on nose.	200	325	550	6
Without "6220" stamped on nose.	125	200	350	3
6250 SEABOARD NW-2: 1954-55, painted blue and orange.				
Decal "SEABOARD."	200	325	500	4
Rubber-stamped "SEABOARD" lettering.	500	675	1,000	6

6262 Wheel Car

6264 Lumber Car

6311 Flatcar with Pipes

6315 Gulf Tank Car

	VG	EX	LN	RARITY
Rubber stamped, with wide spaced lettering (about 2-13/16 to 2-23/32 inches long).	175	275	375	4

6257 LIONEL-SP CABOOSE: 1948-52.

	VG	EX	LN	RARITY
Painted red, red-orange or tile red.	2	5	8	1
Painted dark tile red, as was the smokejack.	200	400	650	7

6257X LIONEL-SP CABOOSE: 1948 only, painted tile-red, equipped with TWO magnetic couplers rather than the usual one. The number 6247X appeared only on its original box. Because the car itself is easily replicated from a 6257, it MUST have its original box to realize the values shown.

	VG	EX	LN	RARITY
	15	25	35	5

6257 LIONEL CABOOSE: 1953-55, unpainted red body.

	VG	EX	LN	RARITY
	5	8	10	1
Painted red, tile red or dark red.	10	18	25	2
1956, double-circled L logo was eliminated.	10	15	22	2

6257-100 LIONEL LINES CABOOSE: 1963-64, unpainted red body, white heat-stamped lettering. Includes die-cast smokejack.

	VG	EX	LN	RARITY
	15	25	40	4

6262 WHEEL CAR: 1956-57, originally furnished with six wheel and axle sets.

	VG	EX	LN	RARITY
Unpainted red body.	400	1,000	1,600	7
Unpainted black body.	50	75	100	4

6264 LUMBER CAR: 1957-58, unpainted red body came with twelve 264-11 timbers retained by eight 2411-4 spring-steel posts.

	VG	EX	LN	RARITY
With bar-end metal trucks.	30	50	75	5
With AAR-type trucks.	40	65	90	6

6311 FLATCAR WITH PIPES: 1955 only, unpainted brown, cargo was three silver-gray plastic pipes, retained by six 2411-4 spring steel posts.

	VG	EX	LN	RARITY
	20	40	65	4

6315 GULF TANK CAR: 1956-58, with flat burnt-orange bands painted on the ends.

	VG	EX	LN	RARITY
	25	55	80	2
Glossy burnt-orange paint.	50	95	150	5
Semi-gloss burnt-orange bands.	40	75	125	4
True orange bands.	60	125	175	5

6346 Alcoa Covered Hopper

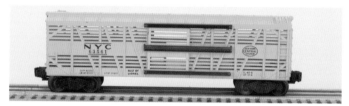

6356 NYC Stock Car

6357 Lionel-SP Caboose

6357 Lionel Caboose

	VG	EX	LN	RARITY
6315 LIONEL LINES TANK CAR: 1963-66, all-orange tank.				
Painted.	75	125	225	6
Unpainted.	10	20	40	3
6315 GULF: 1968-69, unpainted orange tank, no "built date."	20	35	75	4
Rubber stamped "BLT 1-56."	25	45	90	5
6342 NYC CULVERT GONDOLA: 1956-58, 1966-69.				
Dark red body marked "NEW 2-49," metal trucks.	15	25	40	4
Light red body; marked "NEW 2-49," AAR trucks.	15	25	40	3
Medium red body; no "NEW 2-49" markings, AAR trucks.	15	25	40	3
6343 BARREL RAMP CAR: 1961-62.	25	40	65	4
6346 ALCOA COVERED HOPPER: 1956, painted silver, multi-colored ALCOA marking was adhesive-backed paper label, heat-stamped blue lettering.	30	50	75	3
Black heat-stamped lettering.	125	175	250	6
Heat-stamped red lettering.	500	800	1,400	7
6352 PACIFIC FRUIT EXPRESS BOXCAR: 1955-57, unpainted orange body with black heat-stamped lettering; four lines of data rubber stamped on ice compartment door.	75	100	150	4
Three lines of data rubber stamped on ice compartment door.	90	150	250	6
6356 NYC STOCK CAR: 1954-55, painted yellow, rubber-stamped markings.	50	75	100	6
Heat-stamped markings.	25	35	50	4
6357 LIONEL-SP CABOOSE: 1948-53, painted red or tile red.				
Without smokejack.	15	22	35	4
Tuscan or maroon, with black die-cast smoke-jacks.	15	22	35	4
6357 LIONEL CABOOSE: 1953-61.				
Tuscan or maroon, with black die-cast smoke-jacks.	15	22	35	4

6357-50 A. T. & S. F. Caboose

6362 Railway Truck Car

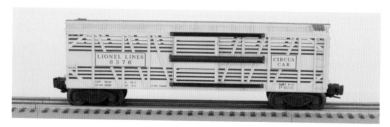

6376 Circus Stock Car

6404 Flatcar with Automobile

	VG	EX	LN	RARITY
Maroon body and maroon smokejack.	275	425	650	7
No double-circle Lionel "L" logo.	15	25	35	3
6357-50 A. T. & S. F. CABOOSE: 1960 only, painted red with white heat-stamped markings.	600	1,000	1,900	8
6361 TIMBER TRANSPORT CAR: 1960-61, 1964-66, and 1968-69, unpainted dark green body; stamped in dull white, black-oxide chains.	40	75	125	4
Lighter green unlettered body, natural gold-color chain.	75	135	210	6
6362 RAILWAY TRUCK CAR: 1955-57, unpainted orange; shiny orange body, bold serif lettering.	30	45	75	4
Unpainted shiny with sans-serif lettering.	30	45	75	4
Pale orange.	125	175	275	7
6376 CIRCUS STOCK CAR: 1956-57, unpainted white plastic, with red trim and markings.	60	100	175	5
6401 FLATCAR: 1965, unpainted gray body.	2	5	10	1
6402 FLATCAR WITH REELS: 1962, 1964-66, 1969.				
Unpainted gray plastic body with orange or light gray reels.	8	13	20	3
Brown plastic body with orange or light gray reels.	8	13	20	3
6402 FLATCAR WITH BOAT: 1969, 6801-75 boat with blue hull.	50	65	100	6
6404 FLATCAR WITH AUTOMOBILE: black plastic body heat stamped "6404" and "BUILT BY LIONEL" in white, with yellow auto with gray bumpers.	40	60	85	6
With red auto with gray bumpers.	40	60	85	6
With a Kelly green auto with gray bumpers.	150	200	275	8
With dark brown auto with gray bumpers.	150	200	275	8
6405 FLATCAR WITH VAN: 1961, heat stamped "6405" furnished with a yellow plastic van with single rear wheels.	20	35	60	5
6406 FLATCAR WITH AUTO: 1961, gray or maroon plastic, unlettered flatcar carrying a single yellow automobile with gray bumpers.	50	75	100	6

6407 Flatcar with Missile

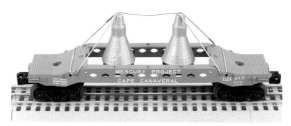

6413 Mercury Capsule Carrying Car

6414 Evans Auto Loader

6414-85 Evans Auto Loader

	VG	EX	LN	RARITY
6407 FLATCAR WITH MISSILE: 1963, with a large missile with removable Mercury capsule produced by Sterling Plastics. The Sterling Plastics name ALWAYS was molded into the base of the capsules.	300	500	700	7
6408 FLATCAR WITH PIPES: 1963, unpainted red plastic flatcar with five gray plastic pipes held on with a rubber band.	15	25	35	4
6409-25 FLATCAR WITH PIPES: 1963, unpainted red plastic flatcar with three gray plastic pipes held on with a rubber band.	15	25	35	4
6411 FLATCAR: 1948-50, medium-gray flatcar with three seven-inch long wooden 3/8-inch dowels.	20	30	40	3
6413 MERCURY CAPSULE CARRYING CAR: 1962-63, unpainted blue body.	100	150	210	5
Painted blue.	150	200	300	6
Unpainted blue-green body.	300	400	600	8
6414 EVANS AUTO LOADER: 1955-66, unpainted red body, black sheet metal superstructure with four 4-5/16-inch-long plastic automobiles. Metal trucks and one each red, white, yellow and green automobiles.	75	110	165	4
AAR-type trucks with one each red, white, yellow and green automobiles.	70	100	150	4
"6414" to the left of "LIONEL," four red autos with gray bumpers.	100	150	200	5
"6414" to the left of "LIONEL," four yellow autos with gray bumpers.	200	300	500	5
"6414" to the left of "LIONEL," four Kelly green autos with gray bumpers.	650	1,000	1,400	8
"6414" to the left of "LIONEL," four brown autos with gray bumpers.	650	1,000	1,400	8
Decaled "6414 AUTO LOADER" legend, four light red automobiles with gray bumpers.	200	400	650	8
6414-85 EVANS AUTO LOADER: 1964, two yellow and two red automobiles adaptations from Lionel's slot cars with molded-in tires.	400	600	900	7
6415 SUNOCO TANK CAR: 1953-55, 1964-66, and 1969, capacity 6,600 gallons, bar-end trucks.	10	17	30	3
8,000 gallons, bar-end trucks.	10	20	40	4
6,600 gallons, AAR-trucks.	10	20	40	4

6416 Boat Loader

6417 Pennsylvania
Caboose

6417-50 Lehigh Valley
Caboose

6419-100 N & W
Caboose

	VG	EX	LN	RARITY
6416 BOAT LOADER: 1961-63, with four boats with white-painted hulls, blue-painted cabin, and brown-painted interior.	125	175	250	5
6417 PENNSYLVANIA CABOOSE: 1953-57, stamped "NEW YORK ZONE."	20	30	45	3
Without "NEW YORK ZONE."	200	300	475	7
6417-25 LIONEL LINES CABOOSE: 1954 only.	20	30	55	3
6417-50 LEHIGH VALLEY CABOOSE: 1954 only, painted gray.	75	125	175	5
Painted Tuscan red.	600	1,000	1,700	8
6418 MACHINERY CAR: 1955-57, with two unnumbered black plastic girders with "LIONEL" in raised white letters.	75	100	125	4
With two unnumbered orange plastic girders with "LIONEL" in raised white lettering.	90	115	150	5
Orange girders with "LIONEL" in raised black lettering.	75	100	125	4
Orange girders without the raised "LIONEL" having accent color.	75	100	125	4
Unnumbered orange plastic girders painted light gray.	90	115	150	5
Girders pinkish red-oxide primer color with raised "U.S. STEEL" lettering outlined in black.	90	115	150	5
Girders black with raised "U.S. STEEL" lettering outlined in white.	75	100	125	4
6419 D. L. & W. CABOOSE: 1948-50, 1952-55.	25	35	50	3
6419-25 D. L. & W. CABOOSE: 1954-55, bar-end trucks but only one coupler.	20	35	50	4
6419-50 D. L. & W. CABOOSE: 1956-57, short die-cast smokejack, bar-end trucks and two magnetic couplers.	20	40	60	4
6419-75 D. L. & W. CABOOSE: 1956, identical to the 6419-50, but with one coupler.	25	40	60	4
6419-100 N & W CABOOSE: 1957-58.	100	150	250	6
6420 D. L. & W. CABOOSE: 1948-50, dark-gray, with operating searchlight.	60	100	150	4
6424 TWIN AUTO CAR: 1956-59, unpainted black plastic; with automobiles with chrome bumpers; with bar-end metal trucks, "6424" heat stamped to the right of the lettering.	30	50	75	4
AAR-type trucks, "6424" heat stamped to the right of the lettering.	30	50	75	4

6425 Gulf Tank Car

6427-60 Virginian Caboose

6429 D. L. & W. Caboose

6434 Poultry Dispatch Stock Car

	VG	EX	LN	RARITY
AAR-type trucks, "6424" heat stamped to the left of Lionel.	30	50	75	4
Made with body tooling for the 6805 Radioactive Waste car.	175	300	425	8
6425 GULF TANK CAR: 1956-58.	15	30	50	3
6427 LIONEL LINES CABOOSE: 1954-60, numbered "64273."	20	30	45	3
6427-60 VIRGINIAN CABOOSE: 1958, painted dark blue with yellow heat-stamped lettering.	125	250	500	6
6427-500 PENNSYLVANIA CABOOSE: 1957-58, painted sky blue and was decorated with white heat-stamped lettering, including the number "576427."	200	350	550	6
6428 UNITED STATES MAIL BOXCAR: 1960-61, 1965-66.	25	35	50	3
6429 D. L. & W. CABOOSE: 1963 only.	150	275	475	7
6430 COOPER-JARRETT VAN CAR: 1956-58, unpainted red flatcar with vans.	40	70	100	4
6431 PIGGY-BACK CAR WITH TRAILER TRUCKS AND TRACTOR: 1966, packaged with two trailers and a road tractor. Car heat stamped "6430," with the number "6431" appearing exclusively on the end of the original box.	175	250	375	7
6434 POULTRY DISPATCH STOCK CAR: 1958-59, painted red, illuminated.	45	70	100	4
6436 LEHIGH VALLEY HOPPER: 1955-56, 1966, black open-top hopper.				
Marked "646361," without spreader bar.	50	65	90	6
Marked "646361," with spreader bar.	20	35	50	4
Marked "643625," without spreader bar.	50	75	100	4
Marked "643625," with spreader bar.	20	35	50	3
6436 LEHIGH VALLEY HOPPER (Type V): 1963-68, red, cataloged as 6436-110. No spreader bar, stamped "NEW 3-55" on sides.	35	50	85	4
No spreader bar and no new date markings.	20	30	50	3
With spreader bar, and "NEW 3-55" on sides.	35	50	85	4
6436 LEHIGH VALLEY HOPPER: 1957-58, lilac painted, with maroon heat-stamped lettering numbered "643657."				
Without spreader bar.	325	500	850	6
With spreader.	125	250	400	4

6440 Pullman

6440 Flatcar with Piggy Back Vans

6445 Fort Knox Gold Reserve

6447 Pennsylvania Caboose

	VG	EX	LN	RARITY
6436: 1969 TCA HOPPER (Train Collectors Association): 1969.	75	90	125	4
6437 PENNSYLVANIA CABOOSE: 1961-68.	15	25	40	3
6440 PULLMAN: 1948-49, brown sheet metal.	25	40	70	3
6440 FLATCAR WITH PIGGY BACK VANS: 1961-63, red flatcar with unpainted gray plastic trailers with only single rear wheels and no decoration.	60	100	145	5
6441 OBSERVATION: 1948-49, brown sheet metal.	25	35	60	3
6442 PULLMAN: 1949, brown sheet metal.	30	60	90	3
6443 OBSERVATION: 1949, brown sheet metal.	30	60	90	3
6445 FORT KNOX GOLD RESERVE: 1961-63.	75	125	175	5
6446 N & W COVERED HOPPER: 1954-55, gray-painted body with cover, without spreader-brace holes, marked "546446."	30	45	60	3
Black-painted body with cover, without spreader-brace holes, marked "546446."	30	45	60	3
Black-painted body with cover, with spreader-brace holes, marked "546446."	50	85	140	5
6446 (-25) N & W: 1955-57, 1963, gray-painted body with cover, and without spreader bar holes, marked "644625."	25	40	60	3
Gray-painted body with cover, with spreader bar holes, marked "644625."	45	65	110	5
Black-painted body with cover, without spreader bar holes, marked "644625."	25	40	60	3
Unpainted gray plastic body, which had spreader-bar holes, marked "644625," AAR trucks.	80	125	180	6
6446 LEHIGH VALLEY HOPPER (6446-60): 1963, body painted red, roof and hatches unpainted red.	110	175	275	7
6447 PENNSYLVANIA CABOOSE: 1963 only.	200	325	500	7
6448 TARGET RANGE BOXCAR: 1961-64, red roof and ends and white side panels.	18	25	40	4
White roof and ends and red side panels.	18	25	40	4
6452 PENNSYLVANIA GONDOLA: 1948-49, numbered "6462" on side and rubber stamped "6452" on bottom of the frame.	12	16	25	3
Car side numbered "6452."	12	16	25	3

X6454 Baby Ruth Boxcar

X6454 Erie Boxcar

X6454 NYC Boxcar

6460 Bucyrus Erie Crane

	VG	EX	LN	RARITY
X6454 A. T. & S. F. BOXCAR: 1948, painted orange with black markings.	20	40	60	5
X6454 BABY RUTH BOXCAR: 1948, painted light orange.	125	250	375	7
X6454 ERIE BOXCAR: 1949-52, brown with white markings.	25	45	75	4
X6454 NYC BOXCAR: 1948 only, tan body with white lettering.	20	30	45	3
Brown body with white lettering.	30	50	75	4
Orange body lettered in black.	75	125	200	7
X6454 PENNSYLVANIA BOXCAR: 1949-52, brown.	25	45	75	4
X6454 SOUTHERN PACIFIC BOXCAR: 1949-52, brown; short piece of the outer circle of the Southern Pacific logo missing between the "R" and the "N."	50	75	125	6
Broken circle was fixed.	30	45	70	4
6456 LEHIGH VALLEY: 1948-55, painted black.	8	10	15	1
Painted dull maroon.	8	10	15	1
Painted semi-gloss maroon.	18	25	35	3
Painted gray body.	25	40	55	4
Painted glossy red with white heat-stamped markings.	350	500	800	7
Painted glossy red with yellow heat-stamped markings.	75	110	175	5
6457 LIONEL CABOOSE: 1949-52, Tuscan-painted body and matching plastic smokejack.	20	30	45	2
Tuscan-painted with matching die-cast smokejack.	15	25	35	1
Tuscan- or maroon-painted bodies with black die-cast smokejack.	15	25	35	1
6460 BUCYRUS ERIE CRANE: 1952-54.				
Black.	40	75	95	3
Red.	40	75	125	4
6461 TRANSFORMER CAR: 1949-50, gray die-cast flatcar with black transformer load.	50	75	100	4

6464-1 Western Pacific Boxcar

6464-75 Rock Island

6464-1 Western Pacific
with red lettering

6464-100 Western Pacific

6464-25 Great Northern Boxcar

6461-125 Pacemaker Boxcar

6464-50 Minneapolis & St. Louis

6464-150 Missouri Pacific Boxcar

	VG	EX	LN	RARITY
6462 NEW YORK CENTRAL GONDOLA: 1949-56, painted black.	10	13	16	1
Unpainted black body.	8	10	12	1
Painted tile red.	8	12	15	1
True red painted (not the tile red).	20	28	40	4
Red-orange painted.	10	15	20	3
Unpainted red.	10	15	20	3
Painted green.	15	22	32	3
6462-500 NEW YORK CENTRAL GONDOLA: 1957-58, pink.	150	200	300	5
6463 ROCKET FUEL TANK CAR: 1962-63, painted snow-white with bright red rubber-stamped lettering.	15	25	60	4
6464-1 WESTERN PACIFIC BOXCAR: 1953-54, painted silver ribs on inside of roof, lettering heat stamped in blue.	600	850	1,400	7
Red heat-stamped markings.	975	1,600	2,500	8
Smooth interior of the roof, blue markings.	50	85	110	3
6464-25 GREAT NORTHERN BOXCAR: 1953-54, painted orange with white heat-stamped lettering.	60	75	100	3
6464-50 MINNEAPOLIS & ST. LOUIS: 1953-56, four full columns of rivets to the right of the door.	50	70	100	3
Three full columns of rivets to the right of the door.	750	1,250	2,000	8
6464-75 ROCK ISLAND: 1953-54, 1969, green-painted body.	60	80	100	3
6464-100 WESTERN PACIFIC: 1954-55, silver (see 6464-250 for orange).	100	130	190	5
6464-125 PACEMAKER BOXCAR: 1954-56, red and gray decorated with white.	75	110	150	5
6464-150 MISSOURI PACIFIC BOXCAR: 1954-55, 1957; "Eagle" and "NEW 3 54" were stamped to the right of the door. Single tack board doors with gray stripes were installed on this car.	75	125	160	4
"NEW 3 54" stamped to the left of the door.	75	125	160	4

6464-175 Rock Island

6464-250 Western Pacific Boxcar

6464-200 Pennsylvania Boxcar

6464-275 State of Maine Boxcar

6464-225 Southern Pacific Boxcar

6464-300 Rutland Boxcar

6464-250 Western Pacific Boxcar

	VG	EX	LN	RARITY
The body had horizontal grooves in it to aid in the masking of the blue and gray stripes. The single tack block doors were solid yellow. "NEW 3 54" stamped to the left of the door.	75	125	160	4
Circular Missouri Pacific Lines herald stamped in the panel immediately to the left of the door, all the other cars have this herald in the fourth panel from the left end of the car.	850	1,250	2,000	8
"Eagle" and the circular Missouri Pacific herald noticeably smaller.	75	125	160	4
6464-175 ROCK ISLAND: 1954-55; painted silver; markings heat stamped in blue, four columns of rivets to right of door.	75	110	175	5
Heat-stamped lettering in black.	750	1,000	1,650	8
Three full columns of rivets to the right of the door, lettered in blue.	800	1,250	2,100	8
6464-200 PENNSYLVANIA BOXCAR: 1954-55, 1969, Tuscan-painted doors and body.	75	110	150	5
6464-225 SOUTHERN PACIFIC BOXCAR: 1954-56, second column of rivets from the left end of the car has two interruptions.	750	1,200	2,100	8
Second rivet column has only five rivets.	75	110	150	4
6464-250 WESTERN PACIFIC BOXCAR: 1954, 1966, painted orange with a blue rubber-stamped feather and white rubber-stamped lettering. Erroneously stamped 6464-100.	700	1,000	1,300	8
Stamped 6464-100, second rivet column to the left of the door had five rivets, three at the top and two at the bottom.	500	1,000	1,600	8
Second and third rivet columns each had five rivets.	130	200	275	5
6464-275 STATE OF MAINE BOXCAR: 1955, 1957-59.				
Unpainted white body with grooves, doors unpainted red plastic.	100	165	250	6
Unpainted royal blue body with grooves, doors painted white plastic.	90	150	210	5
Grooved body painted all three colors, doors painted white plastic.	60	90	125	4
No grooves.	60	90	125	4
6464-300 RUTLAND BOXCAR: 1955-56, clear body casting painted green and yellow.	500	750	1,100	7
Rutland herald has a solid dark green background.	2,000	2,700	4,000	8
Molded yellow body, herald with yellow background.	75	125	175	4

6464-325 Baltimore & Ohio Sentinel Boxcar

6464-350 M-K-T Missouri-Kansas-Texas Boxcar

6464-375 Central of Georgia Boxcar

6464-400 Baltimore & Ohio Boxcar

6464-425 New Haven Boxcar

6464-450 Great Northern Boxcar

	VG	EX	LN	RARITY
Lower half of doors painted glossy dark green.	650	1,000	1,500	7
Faint outline of 6352 roof top hatch visible.	450	675	900	6
6464-325 BALTIMORE & OHIO SENTINEL BOXCAR: 1956 only, painted silver and aqua; single tack board doors.	500	700	975	7
Multiple tack boards.	400	625	875	6
6464-350 M-K-T (Missouri-Kansas-Texas) BOXCAR: 1956 only.	200	300	400	5
6464-375 CENTRAL OF GEORGIA BOXCAR: 1956-57, 1966. The interior of the roof was smooth; decoration includes a built date of "3-56."	75	110	150	4
Interior of the roof ribbed, car does NOT have a "built date."	75	110	150	4
Interior of the roof ribbed markings include the "3-56" built date.	1,600	2,250	3,500	8
6464-400 BALTIMORE & OHIO BOXCAR: 1956-57, 1969, marked "BLT 5-54 BY LIONEL."	70	115	160	4
Marked "BLT 2-56 BY LIONEL."	155	225	300	6
Marked "BLT 5-54 BY LIONEL" on one side and "BLT 2-56 BY LIONEL" on the other.	500	850	1,400	8
No built date information stamped on.	70	100	150	4
6464-425 NEW HAVEN BOXCAR: 1956-58, unpainted black body, "N" of the NH logo had only a half serif on top right corner.	35	60	80	3
Unpainted black body, "N" of the NH logo had full serif.	35	60	80	3
Matte-black painted body; "N" of the NH logo had half serif on the top right corner.	35	60	80	3
Matte-black painted body; "N" of the NH logo had a full serif.	35	60	80	3
Painted glossy black "N" of the NH logo a half serif.	35	60	80	3
6464-450 GREAT NORTHERN BOXCAR: 1956-57, 1966, painted olive with broad horizontal orange stripe with yellow delineating stripes; interior of the roof smooth. Lettered "BLT 1-56 BY LIONEL."	75	125	175	4
The interior of the roof was ribbed. Lettered "BLT 1-56 BY LIONEL."	400	600	900	8
Lettered "BLT BY LIONEL," no date stamped.	75	125	175	4

6464-475 Boston & Maine Boxcar

6464-525 Minneapolis &
St. Louis Boxcar

6464-500 Timken Boxcar

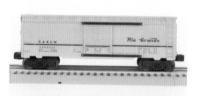

6464-650 Rio Grande Boxcar

6464-510 Pacemaker Boxcar

6464-700 Sante Fe Boxcar

6464-515 M-K-T Boxcar

6464-725 New Haven Boxcar

	VG	EX	LN	RARITY
6464-475 BOSTON & MAINE BOXCAR: 1957-60, 1965-68, interior of roof smooth, stamped "BLT 2-57 BY LIONEL."	30	50	65	3
Interior of roof ribbed, stamped "BLT 2-57 BY LIONEL."	30	50	65	3
Second rivet column to the left of the door had five rivets, no date, only "BLT BY LIONEL."	30	50	65	3
No built date stamped, second and third rivet columns each only five rivets.	75	150	200	6
Second and third rivet columns each only five rivets, stamped "BLT 2-57 BY LIONEL."	65	125	175	5
6464-500 TIMKEN BOXCAR: 1957-59, 1969, yellow, or yellow-orange plastic, stamped "BLT 3-57 BY LIONEL," smooth roof interior.	75	125	175	4
Gray plastic, painted both yellow and white, stamped "BLT 3-57 BY LIONEL," smooth roof interior.	300	275	450	6
Ribbed roof interior, stamped "BLT 3-57 BY LIONEL."	150	200	275	5
Ribbed roof interior, no built date.	75	125	175	4
6464-510 PACEMAKER BOXCAR: 1957-58, pastel blue.	450	675	1,000	7
6464-515 M-K-T BOXCAR: 1957-58, pastel yellow.	450	675	1,000	7
6464-525 MINNEAPOLIS & ST. LOUIS BOXCAR: 1957-58, 1964-66, molded in red plastic, painted red, smooth roof interior.	30	60	100	4
White or marbleized red plastic painted red, ribbed roof interior.	30	60	100	4
Gray plastic painted red.	30	60	100	4
6464-650 RIO GRANDE BOXCAR: 1957-58, 1966, unpainted yellow body molding with silver painted on, including roof, heat stamped "BLT 6-57 BY LIONEL."	75	125	175	4
Unpainted yellow body molding with silver painted on, including roof, heat stamped "BLT BY LIONEL."	75	125	175	4
Gray body casting, with both yellow and silver painted on, roof painted yellow.	1,100	1,600	2,500	8
6464-700 SANTA FE BOXCAR: 1961, 1966, to left of door, the second rivet column had only five rivets.	950	1,500	2,500	8
The second and third left rivet columns each had only five rivets.	80	125	185	4
6464-725 NEW HAVEN BOXCAR: 1962-66, 1968-69, orange, with black door.	40	60	100	3
Black with orange door.	200	275	400	5

6464-825 Alaska Railroad Boxcar

6464-900 New York Central Boxcar

6464-1965 Train Collectors
Association Boxcar

6468 Baltimore & Ohio Boxcar

6468 Baltimore and Ohio - Tuscan

	VG	EX	LN	RARITY
6464-825 ALASKA RAILROAD BOXCAR: 1959-60, doors of authentic cars are always blue. Left of the door, second rivet column had only five rivets.	175	275	375	5
Second and third rivet columns to the left of the door each had only five rivets.	250	375	550	6
6464-900 NEW YORK CENTRAL BOXCAR: 1960-66, body painted jade green. Green doors, left of the door, second rivet column had only five rivets.	900	1,350	1,900	8
Green doors, second and third rivet columns to the left of the door each had only five rivets.	75	125	175	4
Light jade green with unpainted black multiple tack board doors.	50	110	150	6
6464-1965 TRAIN COLLECTORS ASSOCIATION BOXCAR: 1965, uncataloged commemorative for the 1965 TCA convention in Pittsburgh, painted blue body.	80	200	250	8
6465 SUNOCO TANK CAR: 1948-56, two-dome painted silver, technical data ends with the word "TANK."	5	10	15	1
Distinct gray cast.	15	20	35	4
Last line of technical data ends with "6465."	10	15	25	4
6465 GULF/LIONEL LINES TANK CAR: 1958, unpainted gray plastic with the lettering rubber stamped in blue.	15	18	25	3
Molded black body and white rubber-stamped lettering.	40	55	85	4
Painted black with white rubber-stamped lettering.	45	75	110	5
6465 LIONEL LINES TANK CAR: 1959, 1963-66, unpainted black body with white rubber-stamped lettering.	15	40	55	4
Orange.	4	8	12	1
6465 CITIES SERVICE TANK CAR: 1960-62, painted green.	15	25	35	3
6467 MISCELLANEOUS FLATCAR: 1956 only, molded red plastic body white heat-stamped "LIONEL 6467." Unpainted black plastic bulkhead, four spring-steel 2411-4 posts, no load furnished.	30	45	70	4
6468 BALTIMORE & OHIO BOXCAR: 1953-55, painted blue, either glossy or flat.	40	65	100	4
Painted Tuscan.	225	350	500	7

6468-25 New Haven Boxcar

6473 Horse Transport Car

6475 Pickles

6475 Libby's Crushed Pineapple

	VG	EX	LN	RARITY
6468-25 NEW HAVEN BOXCAR: 1956-58, orange body, black doors; "N" of the New Haven logo stamped in black. The "N" sometimes appears with a full serif, other times with a half serif, but both are equally common.	50	75	110	4
Half-serif "N" of the logo heat stamped in white.	150	225	325	6
Tuscan doors.		NOT LEGITIMATE		
6469 LIQUIFIED GAS CAR: 1963 only. Unpainted red plastic with orange tint, heat-stamped "Lionel" in white, black molded plastic bulkheads glued in place. The load was a cardboard tube wrapped in glossy white paper. On it, printed in black, was the car number "6469" and an Erie herald. Sheet metal caps were painted white and crimped on each end of the tube.	40	90	150	5
6470 EXPLOSIVES BOXCAR: 1959-60.	30	50	70	4
6472 REFRIGERATOR: 1950-53.	25	35	50	4
6473 HORSE TRANSPORT CAR: 1962-66, 1969.	25	35	50	3
6475 PICKLES: 1960-62, without the hoop and stave stamping, but with the red "Pickles."	35	50	85	4
With hoop and stave stamping, and "Pickles" lettering.	25	45	65	3
6475 LIBBY'S CRUSHED PINEAPPLE: 1963-64, vats covered in adhesive silver paper with Libby's logos.				
Aqua body.	50	60	85	4
Medium-blue body.	30	40	60	3
6476 LEHIGH VALLEY HOPPER: 1957-69, early 1957 production equipped with metal trucks, remainder of the production used AAR trucks.				
Red.	10	16	22	2
Gray.	10	16	22	2
Black.	10	16	22	2
6476-1 TOY TRAIN OPERATING SOCIETY HOPPER: 1969 only, uncataloged.	40	65	110	5
6476 LEHIGH VALLEY: 1959-63, medium red opaque body. No number on car.	8	10	15	1

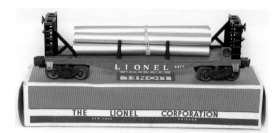

6477 Miscellaneous Car with Pipes

6500 Beechcraft Bonanza Transport Car

6500 Beechcraft Bonanza Transport Car

6501 Flatcar with Motorboat

	VG	EX	LN	RARITY
Light translucent red body.	8	10	15	1
Dark translucent red body.	8	10	15	1
Coral-pink opaque body.	15	30	50	4
Black.	15	25	45	4

6476-135 LEHIGH VALLEY: 1964-66, 1968, listed in various catalogs was a yellow 6476 hopper. Be advised, however, that no yellow hopper cars were produced with the number "6476" stamped on them. Rather, the 6476 number denoted two operating couplers. The cars themselves used various black Lehigh Valley heat stamps, with various numbers and built and new dates.   **SEE OTHER LISTINGS**

6477 MISCELLANEOUS CAR WITH PIPES: 1957-58, molded red plastic body with unpainted black plastic bulkheads and four spring-steel 2411-4 posts, with a load of five silver-gray plastic pipes.

	VG	EX	LN	RARITY
	30	60	80	4

6480 EXPLOSIVES BOXCAR: 1961 only.

	VG	EX	LN	RARITY
	30	50	70	4

6482 REFRIGERATOR: 1957 only, always had sprung plastic doors.

	VG	EX	LN	RARITY
	40	55	85	5

6500 BEECHCRAFT BONANZA TRANSPORT CAR: 1962, unnumbered, unpainted black flatcar. Airplane secured using a 6418-9 elastic band. Airplane heat stamped with "BONANZA" on each side and the FAA registration number "N2742B" on one wing. Lionel New York identification molded into underside of fuselage. Four rivets bind each wing together. White lettering, red upper wings and fuselage. The lower fuselage half and propeller were white.

	VG	EX	LN	RARITY
	425	550	800	6
Others had white upper surfaces, red lower surfaces and a red propeller.	550	700	1,000	7

6501 FLATCAR WITH MOTORBOAT: 1962-63, with a small plastic boat that was propelled through the water by pellets of baking soda, supplied with the car in a foil packet of forty.

	VG	EX	LN	RARITY
	90	125	175	5

6502 STEEL GIRDER TRANSPORT CAR: 1962-63, with a single unpainted orange girder with "LIONEL" in raised lettering retained by a 6418-9 elastic band.

	VG	EX	LN	RARITY
Unpainted black plastic body.	20	35	60	5
Unpainted red plastic body.	50	80	125	6

6511 Pipe Car

6512 Cherry Picker Car

6517-75 Erie Caboose

6518 Transformer Car

	VG	EX	LN	RARITY
6502-50 STEEL GIRDER TRANSPORT CAR: Circa 1963. Unlettered, unpainted blue plastic car payload was single unpainted orange girder with "LIONEL" in raised lettering retained by a 6418-9 elastic band.	25	40	60	5
6511 PIPE CAR: 1953-56, furnished with five standard silver-gray plastic pipes and a small envelope containing thirteen 2411-4 spring steel posts. Molded of black plastic painted dark red. Die-cast plates on the underside of each end of the car served as attachment points for the trucks.	25	50	75	5
Painted a dull brick red with die-cast plates.	25	50	75	5
Painted dark red with blued-steel plates.	20	40	60	3
Unpainted light brown body with blued-steel plates.	20	45	65	4
Unpainted reddish brown with blued-steel plates.	20	40	60	3
6512 CHERRY PICKER CAR: 1962-63.	75	100	175	5
6517 LIONEL LINES CABOOSE: 1955-59.				
Underscoring beneath "BLT 12-55" and "LIONEL."	40	75	100	5
No underscoring.	35	60	80	4
6517-75 ERIE CABOOSE: 1966 only.	250	425	575	7
6517/1966 TCA CABOOSE: 1966, uncataloged commemorative.	75	125	200	7
6518 TRANSFORMER CAR: 1956-58, upper transformer panel heat stamped in white "6518," lower panel was heat stamped "LIONEL TRANSFORMER CAR."	75	125	165	5
6519 ALLIS-CHALMERS HEAT EXCHANGER CAR: 1958-61, molded medium-orange plastic.	55	85	125	4
Dark-orange plastic.	55	85	125	4
Milky-orange colored plastic.	100	150	225	6
6520 LIONEL LINES: 1949-51, simulated generator hid an off-on switch that could be actuated with a remote control uncoupling track. Beware of reproduction generators.				
Tan generator.	300	550	750	8
Green generator.	225	350	475	6

6530 Firefighting Instruction Car

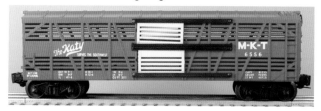

6556 M-K-T Stock Car

6557 Lionel Smoking Caboose

656025 Bucyrus Erie

	VG	EX	LN	RARITY
Orange generator.	30	50	75	3
Maroon generator.	40	75	100	4
6530 FIREFIGHTING INSTRUCTION CAR: 1960-62, unpainted red plastic body and unpainted white plastic opening doors.	65	100	150	5
6536 M & St. L HOPPER (Minneapolis & St. Louis): 1958-59, 1963, large open-topped hopper.	35	55	85	4
6544 MISSILE FIRING CAR: 1960-64, came with two small envelopes, each containing four 44-40 rockets. Control panel heat stamped in white.	100	140	225	4
Control panel heat stamped in black.	225	375	600	6
6555 SUNOCO TANK CAR: 1949-50, tank painted silver.				
Sunoco decal with "GAS" above and "OILS" below "SUNOCO" in the herald.	20	40	65	4
Without the "GAS/OILS" in the herald.	20	40	65	4
6556 M-K-T STOCK CAR: 1958 only.	150	250	450	7
6557 LIONEL SMOKING CABOOSE: 1958-59, "6557" stamped on the left end of the car.	150	250	400	6
"6557" stamped on the right-hand end of the body.	200	350	550	7
6560 BUCYRUS ERIE CRANE: 1955-64, 1966-69, equipped with metal trucks mounted using binding head screws and spacer rings.	100	185	275	5
Gray cab, no spacer rings, metal trucks, crank wheels had opened spokes.	60	80	125	4
Molded red cab open spoke crank wheels, metal trucks.	30	45	60	3
Red cab, no number on frame, metal trucks, open spoke crank wheels.	50	70	90	4
Red cab, AAR-type trucks, open spoke crank wheels.	30	45	65	3
Red cab, AAR-type trucks, solid crank wheels.	30	45	65	3
Red cab, dark blue frame.	50	85	125	4
656025 BUCYRUS ERIE: 1956, red cab, frame heat stamped "656025."	65	115	170	5
6561 CABLE REEL CAR: 1953-56, reels wound with solid aluminum wire; gray unpainted plastic reels.	55	90	125	5

6572 Railway Express Agency Refrigerator

6640 U. S. M. C. Missile Launching Car

6651 U.S. Marine Corps Cannon Firing Car

6657 Rio Grande Caboose

	VG	EX	LN	RARITY
Unpainted orange plastic reels.	45	70	110	4

6562 NEW YORK CENTRAL GONDOLA: 1956-58, usually included a load of four red canisters with "Lionel Air Activated Container" lettering.

	VG	EX	LN	RARITY
Gray.	28	45	60	4
Red.	28	45	60	4
Black.	28	45	60	4

6572 RAILWAY EXPRESS AGENCY REFRIGERATOR: 1958-59, 1963, painted dark green and equipped with 2400-series passenger car trucks.

	VG	EX	LN	RARITY
	85	135	200	6
Bar-end metal trucks.	80	125	175	5
Light green with AAR-type trucks.	65	95	125	4

6630 MISSILE LAUNCHING CAR: 1961, unpainted black plastic body with pivoting blue plastic launcher base.

	VG	EX	LN	RARITY
	75	110	175	5

6636 ALASKA RAILROAD HOPPER: 1959-60.

	VG	EX	LN	RARITY
	35	55	85	4

6640 U. S. M. C. MISSILE LAUNCHING CAR: 1960, body painted olive drab and was heat stamped "U.S.M.C. 6640" in white. Unpainted olive drab plastic launcher base with a black plastic launch rail.

	VG	EX	LN	RARITY
	150	250	350	7

6646 LIONEL LINES STOCK CAR: 1957 only, orange.

	VG	EX	LN	RARITY
	20	35	55	5

6650 MISSILE LAUNCHING CAR: 1959-63, unpainted red plastic body heat stamped "6650 LIONEL." Pivoting unpainted blue plastic launcher base with a black plastic launch rail.

	VG	EX	LN	RARITY
	35	50	75	4

6651 U.S. MARINE CORPS CANNON FIRING CAR: 1964-65.

	VG	EX	LN	RARITY
	125	250	350	6

6656 LIONEL LINES STOCK CAR: 1950-53, bright yellow with adhesive-backed "Armour" emblem applied to their doors.

	VG	EX	LN	RARITY
	45	75	120	5
Bright yellow without "Armour" emblem.	18	25	35	3
Dark yellow without "Armour" emblem.	18	25	35	3

6657 RIO GRANDE CABOOSE: 1957-58, body molded with slots in the roof overhang to accept ladders, which were not installed.

	VG	EX	LN	RARITY
	75	125	225	5
Body molded without the ladder slots.	125	200	375	7

6660 Boom Car

6736 Detroit & Mackinac Hopper

6800 Airplane Car

6801-50 Boat Car

	VG	EX	LN	RARITY
6660 BOOM CAR: 1958, equipped with a pair of outriggers.	50	75	115	5
6670 DERRICK CAR: 1959-60, no outriggers.	40	60	90	4
6672 SANTA FE REFRIGERATOR: 1954-56, three lines of data to the right of the door and blue heat-stamped lettering.	150	250	425	7
Either black or blue lettering with two lines of data to right of door.	45	75	100	4
Black lettering, no circled-L Lionel logo.	45	75	100	4
6736 DETROIT & MACKINAC HOPPER: 1960-62; face of the figure in Mackinac Mac clear.	25	50	80	3
Face of Mackinac Mac partially obliterated.	25	50	80	3
6800 AIRPLANE CAR: 1957-60, unpainted red flatcar, undecorated yellow and black plastic aircraft with identifying markings molded into the underside of the fuselage. These markings read, "NO. 6800-60 AIRPLANE THE LIONEL CORPORATION NEW YORK, N.Y. MADE IN U.S. OF AMERICA."				
Either black upper surfaces and yellow propeller or yellow upper surfaces with black propeller. Only three rivets to bind the wing halves. Car equipped with metal trucks.	125	200	325	5
Equipped with AAR-type trucks number stamped to the right of "LIONEL."	125	200	325	5
Equipped with AAR-type trucks number stamped to the left of "LIONEL."	125	200	325	5
6801 BOAT CAR: 1957-60, unpainted red flatcar with boat secured in an unpainted gray plastic cradle by 6418-9 elastic band. Metal trucks, white-hulled boat with a brown deck that had no Lionel markings.	70	100	150	4
AAR-type trucks, white-hulled boat with a brown deck that had no Lionel markings.	70	100	150	4
6801-50 BOAT CAR: AAR-type trucks, boat with yellow hull marked "NO. 6801-60 BOAT MADE IN U.S. OF AMERICA" to the right of the engine hatch and "THE LIONEL CORPORATION NEW YORK, N.Y."	70	100	150	4
6801-75 BOAT CAR: AAR-type trucks, boat with blue hull marked "NO. 6801-60 BOAT MADE IN U.S. OF AMERICA" to the right of the engine hatch and "THE LIONEL CORPORATION NEW YORK, N.Y." on the left.	70	100	150	4
6802 FLATCAR WITH GIRDERS: 1958-59, molded red flatcar with two black plastic "U.S. STEEL" girders secured with a 6418-9 elastic band. Car heat stamped "6802 LIONEL."	20	25	35	4

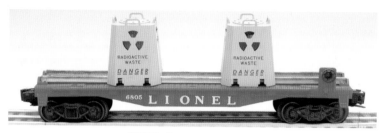

6805 Radioactive Waste Car

6806 Flatcar with Military Units

6808 Flatcar with Military Load

6809 Flatcar with Military Units

	VG	EX	LN	RARITY
6803 FLATCAR WITH MILITARY UNITS: 1958-59, hauled a tank and a truck with swiveling loudspeakers, both heat stamped with U.S. Marine Corps markings.	125	200	325	6
6804 FLATCAR WITH MILITARY UNITS: 1958-59, one truck with swiveling twin anti-aircraft guns and a second truck with swiveling loudspeakers. U.S.M.C. markings on vehicles.	125	200	325	6
6805 RADIOACTIVE WASTE CAR: 1958-59, with two illuminated painted gray simulated concrete radioactive waste containers.	75	135	200	5
6806 FLATCAR WITH MILITARY UNITS: 1958-59, cargo was a medical truck and a truck with a swiveling radar antenna.	100	175	300	6
6807 FLATCAR WITH DUKW: 1958-59, cargo was amphibious 2-1/2 ton 6x6 truck.	75	100	150	5
6808 FLATCAR WITH MILITARY LOAD: 1958-59, carried a truck with a searchlight and a replica of an M-19 Gun Motor Carriage with twin 40mm Bofors anti-aircraft cannon.	200	275	400	6
6809 FLATCAR WITH MILITARY UNITS: 1958-59, carried a medical van and truck with swiveling twin anti-aircraft guns.	125	200	300	6
6810 FLATCAR WITH COOPER-JARRETT VAN: 1958, carried one white trailer with black and copper-colored Cooper-Jarrett signs.	35	50	70	5
6812 TRACK MAINTENANCE CAR: 1959-61, body unpainted red plastic heat stamped "6812" to the left of "LIONEL" in white serif letters. All three plastic components of their superstructure molded in matching black plastic.	50	80	125	4
Black superstructure base with a gray platform and crank handle.	50	80	125	4
Gray superstructure base with black platform and crank handle.	50	80	125	4
All three superstructure components molded gray plastic.	50	80	125	4
All three superstructure components molded bright lemon yellow plastic.	50	80	125	4
All three superstructure components molded dark yellow plastic.	80	125	150	5
All three superstructure components molded of cream-colored plastic.	100	200	275	7

6814 Rescue Unit

6816 Flatcar with Allis-Chalmers Crawler Tractor

	VG	EX	LN	RARITY
6814 RESCUE UNIT: 1959-61, referred to by the catalog as a First Aid Medical Car, it included a tool compartment insert, two molded plastic stretchers and oxygen tank, and a blue rubber figure. All the plastic components were painted white with red heat-stamped markings, including red crosses on the stretchers. The sheet metal frame was painted gray.	50	100	165	5

6816 FLATCAR WITH ALLIS-CHALMERS CRAWLER TRACTOR: 1959-60.

The earliest dozer (Type I) was believed to have been molded in dark orange plastic. "ALLIS-CHALMERS" was heat stamped on the back of the seat in white while the "TORQUE CONVERTER" emblem was heat stamped in black on each side of the seat. The raised "ALLIS-CHALMERS" molded alongside the hood was picked out in black. Lionel soon discontinued the black highlighting of the lettering on the hood, resulting in the first variation in the design. We will call this the Type II tractor.

The next variation (Type III) came about when "HD 16 DIESEL" was stamped in black above the torque converter emblem on the seat sides.

The Type IV was identical to the Type III except the rear drawbar was shortened and its holes filled in.

When production of the Type V tractor began the seat back lettering was changed to black. The final version (Type VI) was made of a considerably lighter orange plastic than the other vehicles.

In addition to being packaged with the flatcar, this bulldozer was also offered for separate sale by Lionel packaged in an orange picture box, and by Allis-Chalmers, who had it packed in a striped box.

	VG	EX	LN	RARITY
Most of these flatcars had unpainted red plastic bodies. If found with a Type I or Type VI dozer, a 50 percent premium should be added to the values shown here.	300	475	700	6
Unpainted black plastic bodies. Once again, a Type I or Type II dozer would increase the values shown below.	1,000	1,800	3,200	8

6817 Flatcar with Allis-Chalmers Scraper

6820 Aerial Missile Transport Car

	VG	EX	LN	RARITY

6817 FLATCAR WITH ALLIS-CHALMERS SCRAPER: 1959-60, with orange articulated Allis-Chalmers scraper retained with a 6418-9 elastic band.

Two versions of the unpainted orange plastic scraper load were produced. The earliest Type I version had a windshield frame made of wire installed and had "ALLIS CHALMERS" heat-stamped in white on the scraper frame, and the raised "ALLIS CHALMERS" on the tractor hood picked out in black.

The later Type II version lacked the wire windshield frame and had no colorful markings. The grille molding was modified as well. This version is much more abundant than the early version.

The scraper was also available for separate sale through Lionel outlets, though packaged in a plain white box, or through Allis-Chalmers in a striped box. Also like the bulldozer, the scraper was fragile and is often found broken. The usual victims are the exhaust stack, the pin that couples the tractor to the scraper (this is often repaired with an insulating track pin), or again as with the bulldozer, the hydraulic cylinders.

	VG	EX	LN	RARITY
Unpainted flatcar. The prices shown below are predicated on the Type II scraper. If the Type I load is substituted, add a 30 percent premium.	350	450	700	6
Unpainted black flatcar.	1,250	2,500	4,000	8

6818 FLATCAR WITH TRANSFORMER: 1958, transformer heat stamped "6818" on the upper panel, and "LIONEL TRANSFORMER CAR" was heat stamped on the lower panel in white.

	VG	EX	LN	RARITY
	35	50	70	5

6819 FLATCAR WITH HELICOPTER: 1959-61, intended to be supplied with a non-operating helicopter, although occasionally they surface with an operating helicopter which was probably a substitution due to material shortages at Lionel. The non-operating helicopter had a gray fuselage and an opaque yellow tail rotor, it came both unmarked and heat stamped "NAVY."

	VG	EX	LN	RARITY
	50	75	125	5

6820 AERIAL MISSILE TRANSPORT CAR: 1960-61, helicopter equipped with two huge, non-firing missiles.

	VG	EX	LN	RARITY
	150	250	400	7

6823 Flatcar with I. R. B. M. Missiles

6824 U. S. M. C. Caboose

6826 Flatcar with Christmas Trees

6827 P & H Power Shovel Car

	VG	EX	LN	RARITY
6821 FLATCAR WITH CRATES: 1959-60, cargo was a modification of the crate load created for the 3444 animated gondola. Occasionally this car surfaces with a shorter version of the crate load, but the short load was used on an HO-Gauge car and is not correct in this application.	20	30	50	4
6822 NIGHT CREW SEARCHLIGHT: 1961-69, superstructure gray plastic and searchlight housing black.	25	40	70	4
Superstructure black plastic and searchlight housing gray.	25	40	70	4
6823 FLATCAR WITH I.R.B.M. MISSILES: 1959-60, carried two 6650-type missiles. Each missile is supported by a 6801-64 boat cradle, and retained by 6418-9 silver elastic bands. Both missiles in the pair matched and could be red over white, white over red or all white.	40	65	100	5
6824 U. S. M. C. CABOOSE: 1960, cab, tool compartment, tool compartment insert and frame were all painted olive drab. The markings were all done in white: "U.S.M.C." rubber stamped on the sheet metal frame and "RESCUE UNIT," "6824" and two crosses heat stamped on the plastic components. The First-Aid Medical Car had a short black die-cast smokejack, a blue rubber figure with painted hands and face, a white plastic air tank, and two white plastic stretchers with Red Cross markings.	125	200	325	7
6824-50 FIRST AID CABOOSE: 1964, did not have crewman, tool compartment insert, stretchers, or oxygen tank; frame was black with white heat-stamped sans-serif lettering.	50	100	150	7
6825 FLATCAR WITH ARCH TRESTLE BRIDGE: 1959-62, bridges can be found in both black and gray, although it is believed that only the black is the correct load for the flatcar, although a car with the gray HO bridge makes a nice companion piece. Number was heat stamped to the left of "LIONEL."	30	50	90	4
Number was heat stamped to the right of "LIONEL."	30	50	90	4
6826 FLATCAR WITH CHRISTMAS TREES: 1959-60, with four spring-steel 2411-4 posts to keep the foliage load in place.	100	150	225	5
6827 P & H POWER SHOVEL CAR: 1960-63, black flatcar was heat-stamped "6827" to the left of "LIONEL" in white. Power shovel came as a kit in its own yellow, black and white box packed with car in orange Lionel box.	125	200	300	6

6828 P & H Mobile Construction Crane Car

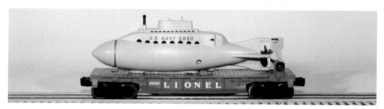

6830 Submarine Car

6844 Missile Carrying Car

Unnumbered Flatcar

	VG	EX	LN	RARITY
6828 P & H MOBILE CONSTRUCTION CRANE CAR: 1960-63, 1966, load was a kit of a crane produced by the Harnischfeger Corp. This kit, in its own yellow and black P & H box, was packaged along with the flatcar inside a Lionel box. Flatcar was unpainted black plastic.	150	250	350	6
Unpainted red plastic flatcar.	500	700	1,200	8
6830 SUBMARINE CAR: 1960-61, with a non-operating Lionel submarine with 6830 black heat-stamped number on sub.	100	140	200	6
6844 MISSILE CARRYING CAR: 1959-60, rack held six white 44-40 missiles.				
Unpainted black plastic frames.	45	70	110	5
Unpainted red plastic frames.	600	800	1,400	8

UNNUMBERED FLATCAR: Gray unpainted 1877-style flatcar with no markings, no truss rods and AAR-type trucks. Carried either a moss-green tank or moss-green Jeep and cannon, made by Payton Plastics.

There is not sufficient information to determine market value, however, an authentic load is key to its scarcity.

UNMARKED HOPPER: 1963-69, short hopper.

	VG	EX	LN	RARITY
Bright yellow.	30	40	50	5
Dark yellow.	15	20	30	4
Red body.	30	45	60	5
Black body.	30	45	60	5
Gray body.	15	18	25	3
Olive body.	50	75	110	6

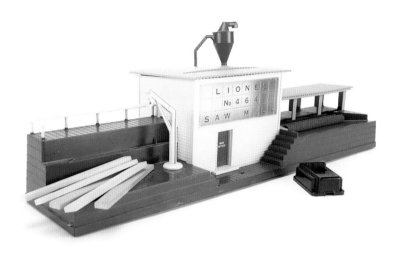

Accessories, Track

One of the key elements in Lionel's success, both pre and postwar was their numerous operating accessories. Joshua Cowen felt it was important to provide a means for children and adults to interact with the trains, as well as provide a semi-realistic setting to operate them in.

Initially the postwar accessories were carryovers of their prewar counterparts. The 45 Gateman, 115 Station, 313 Bascule Bridge, 97 and 164 Coal and Lumber Loaders were all introduced before WWII. Soon however, new designs poured from the Lionel shops. The 132 Station, 397 Coal Loader and 364 Lumber Loader, all less expensive to produce than their prewar designed counterparts pushed the earlier models from the catalog.

More than any other component, the development of the vibrator motor allowed Lionel to create a bewildering array of animated yet inexpensive accessories including operating forklift platforms, animated newsstands, culvert loaders and unloaders.

Not all accessories provided action. Bridges crossed gorges, street lamps illuminated the miniature villages of Lionelville and Plasticville, the latter dotted with buildings sold by Lionel, but made by Bachmann.

and Transformers

Today Lionel's accessories retain their appeal to operators and collectors alike. Children, young or old, still delight in watching day to day tasks performed in miniature by these accessories.

Despite their appeal compared to trains and starter sets in particular, all accessories are relatively scarce. The rarity ratings given in this chapter are relative to other accessories, not the Lionel product line as a whole. Even the most common of accessories like the 145 Gateman is more difficult to locate than a common train car, such as the 6462 Gondola.

Also cataloged as accessories by Lionel were various easily lost loads and a few fragile repair parts. Virtually every part of every item was available through Authorized Lionel Service Stations, but the parts cataloged as accessories were available to any Lionel retail outlet. Whereas repair parts typically came in blue and manila envelopes that were hand-labeled as to contents, the "accessory" parts came in conventional retail packaging. It is this retail packaging that warrants the values listed for such items; the items themselves as a rule are easily located. Representative examples of these accessory items are included in the following listings as well.

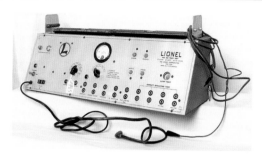

5C Test Set

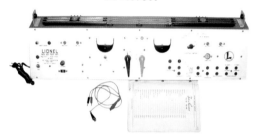

5D Test Set

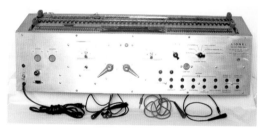

5F Test Set

025 Bumper

	VG	EX	LN	RARITY
5C TEST SET: Equipped to test 0 and 027 locomotives, as well as operating cars and couplers.	Too rarely traded to establish accurate pricing.			
5D TEST SET: Equipped to test 0 and 027 locomotives, as well as operating cars and couplers.	500	800	1,200	7
5F TEST SET: Equipped with Super 0 and HO track.	800	1,500	2,200	2
011-11 INSULATING PINS: The collector value of these O-Gauge pins is in the packaging.	1	2	3	2
011-43 INSULATING PINS: The collector value of these O-Gauge pins is in the packaging.	1	2	3	2
020 90-DEGREE CROSSOVER: Introduced in 1915 and available continuously through 1961.	5	7	10	2
020X 45-DEGREE CROSSING: Introduced in 1915 and available continuously through 1959.	6	9	14	3
022 REMOTE CONTROL SWITCHES: 1945-66, differ from prewar units. Nameplate reads "LIONEL REMOTE CONTROL NO. O22 O GAUGE SWITCH." The pair of turnouts came with a pair of illuminated 022C controllers.	60	75	90	2
022LH REMOTE CONTROL SWITCH: 1950-61, individually sold turnout with controller. Its separate-sale box enhances value.	35	45	55	4
022RH REMOTE CONTROL SWITCH: 1950-61, individually sold turnout with controller. Its separate-sale box enhances value.	35	45	55	4
022A REMOTE CONTROL SWITCH: 1947, these switches were built without fixed voltage capabilities or bottom plates; furnished with a single 1121C-60 control to operate the pair.	100	150	275	8
022-500 O-GAUGE ADAPTER SET: 1957-61, allows the use of O-Gauge switches with Super 0 track. Much of the value is in the packaging.	2	3	4	4
025 BUMPER: 1946-47, illuminated black-painted die-cast bumper attached to a piece of O-Gauge track.	15	20	30	3
26 BUMPER: 1948, gray die-cast housing.	30	40	50	6
1949-50, red die-cast housing.	10	15	25	4
28-6 18-VOLT RED LAMPS: The values listed below are for individual bulbs. When 12-pack box, as shown, is offered the value of the 12-pack is 100 times the value of the individual bulb.	3	4	5	6

30 Water Tower

31 Curved Track

32 Straight Track

35 Boulevard Lamp

	VG	EX	LN	RARITY
30 WATER TOWER: This water tower ultimately replaced the more elaborate 38 tower beginning in 1947, and remained in the catalog through 1950. It had a dark gray die-cast base and a solenoid-lowered plastic spout made from two mirror-image pieces of plastic. The tank was translucent amber plastic lined with Kraft paper.				
30 WATER TOWER: 1947-50, brown supports, gray roof.	100	175	300	5
Black supports, gray roof with hole.	100	175	300	5
Black supports, brown roof.	100	160	275	4
Brown supports, gray roof without hole.	80	125	200	3
31 CURVED TRACK: 1957-66, Super 0.	1	2	4	4
31-7 POWER BLADE CONNECTOR: 1957-60, envelope contains 12 of the copper connectors used on the center rails of Super 0 track. The value here is primarily in the packaging.	1	2	3	3
31-15 GROUND RAIL PIN: 1957-66, package of one dozen pins for use in the outer rails of Super 0 track.	1	2	3	3
31-45 POWER BLADE CONNECTOR: 1961-66, envelope contains 12 of the copper connectors used on the center rails of Super 0 track. The value here is primarily in the packaging.	1	2	3	3
32 STRAIGHT TRACK: 1957-66, more difficult to locate than curved sections.	2	4	6	5
32-10 INSULATING PIN: 1957-60, pack of one dozen insulating pins for use in the outer rails of Super 0 track.	1	2	3	4
32-20 POWER BLADE INSULATOR: 1957-60, pack of one dozen insulating pins for center power blade of Super 0 track.	1	2	3	4
32-45 POWER BLADE INSULATOR: 1961-66, pack of one dozen insulating pins for center power blade of Super 0 track.	1	2	3	4
32-55 INSULATING PIN: 1961-66, one dozen insulating pins for use in the outer rails of Super 0 track.	1	2	3	4
33 HALF CURVED TRACK: 1957-66, half section of Super 0 curved track.	1	2	3	5
34 HALF STRAIGHT TRACK: 1957-66, 5-3/4-inch long half sections of Super 0 straight track.	1	2	3	5
35 BOULEVARD LAMP: 1945-49.	20	35	60	5

36 Operating Car Remote

38 Water Tower

38 Accessory Adapter Tracks

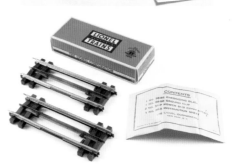

40 Hook Up Wire

	VG	EX	LN	RARITY
36 OPERATING CAR REMOTE CONTROL SET: 1957-66, includes two control blades, a 90 controller and the needed hook up wire.	8	12	18	5
37 UNCOUPLING TRACK SET: 1957-66, 1-1/2-inch long Super 0 track section with a 90 controller and hook up wire.	10	15	20	5
38 WATER TOWER: 1946-47, pumping water tower with turned finial, small funnel and pack of tablets.				
Black supports with brown or gray-painted roof.	275	375	525	7
Brown supports and red-painted roof.	250	325	475	6
38 ACCESSORY ADAPTER TRACKS: 1957-61, pair of special tracks with only four crossties was needed to allow the attachment of track trips such as those coming with the 55 or 3360, or installation on accessory bases, as with the 497 or 3656, to Super 0 track.	8	12	15	4
39-3 12-VOLT FROSTED LAMPS: Replacement lamp individually packed in its own tiny orange and blue "Lionel Trains" box for retail sale. Twelve boxes were packed into a larger orange and blue box for dealer sales. The values listed below are for individual bulbs. When a 12-pack box, as shown, is offered the value of the 12-pack is 100 times the value of the individual bulb.	3	4	5	6
39-25 OPERATING TRACK SET:	10	15	25	5
40 HOOK UP WIRE: 1950-51 and 1953-63, orange or gray reel wrapped with 50 feet of 18-Gauge single conductor wire. Wire was insulated in either yellow, maroon, blue or white plastic.	5	20	45	5
40-3 18-VOLT FROSTED LAMPS: Replacement lamp individually packed in its own tiny orange and blue "Lionel Trains" box for retail sale. Twelve boxes were packed into a larger orange and blue box for dealer sales. The values listed below are for individual bulbs. When a 12-pack box, as shown, is offered the value of the 12-pack is 100 times the value of the individual bulb.	3	4	5	6
40-25 CABLE REEL: 1955-57, and again in 1959. This orange reel holds 15 inches of the same black four-conductor wire as used on Lionel remote control track sections. It came packaged in a preprinted manila envelope, and it is that envelope that actually has the values listed here.	75	175	350	7

45N Automatic Gateman

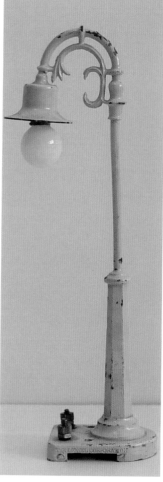

64 Highway Lamppost

58 Lamppost

70 Lamppost

	VG	EX	LN	RARITY
40-50 CABLE REEL: 1960-61, this orange reel holds 15 inches of the same black three-conductor wire as used on Lionel switch controls. It came packaged in a preprinted manila envelope, and it is that envelope that actually has the values listed here.	75	175	350	7
042 MANUAL SWITCHES: 1946-59, pair of illuminated, manually operated O-Gauge turnouts. In 1950, the screw-base 1447 bulb was replaced with a bayonet base 1445.	40	50	60	4
43 POWER TRACK: 1959-66, special 1-1/2-inch track section with built-in fahnstock clips.	5	7	10	3
44-80 MISSILES: 1959-60, set of four replacement missiles for the 44, 45, 6544 and 6844.	10	20	30	7
45 GATEMAN: 1946-49, merely a renumbering of the 1945 45N.	40	50	60	2
45N AUTOMATIC GATEMAN: Prewar and 1945-only postwar.	50	65	80	5
48 INSULATED STRAIGHT TRACK: 1957-66, Super 0 insulated section.	5	7	10	5
49 INSULATED CURVED TRACK: 1957-66, Super 0 insulated section.	5	7	10	5
56 LAMPPOST: Prewar and 1946-49, green.	30	45	60	4
58 LAMPPOST: Prewar and 1946-50, postwar ivory only.	35	50	65	5
61 GROUND LOCKON: 1957-66, special lockon, for outside rail of Super 0 track.	1	2	3	5
62 POWER LOCKON: 1957-66, used to make the electrical connection to the center rail of Super 0 track.	1	2	3	5
64 HIGHWAY LAMPPOST: 1945-49, prewar green, 6-3/4-inch tall lamp used a special bulb.	45	60	75	6
64-15 12-VOLT OPAL LAMPS: 12-pack box of special bulbs for 64 lamppost. The value of the 12-pack is 100 times the value of the individual bulb listed here.	7	10	15	7
70 LAMPPOST: 1949-50, 4-1/2-inch tall lamp with a die-cast tilting head.	25	40	60	4
71 LAMPPOST: 1949-59, six-inch tall gray die-cast lamp with a press-on lamp housing.	15	20	30	3
75 GOOSE NECK LAMPS: 1961-63, pair of 6-1/2-inch tall black plastic lamps.	15	25	40	4
76 BOULEVARD STREET LAMPS: 1956-69, set of three green plastic lamps.	15	25	40	3
88 CONTROLLER: 1946-50, SPST push button normally closed momentary contact switch.	1	2	10	2

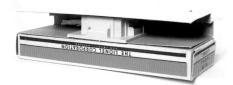

89 Flagpole

93 Water Tower

97 Coal Elevator

110 Trestle Set

	VG	EX	LN	RARITY
89 FLAGPOLE: 1956-58, fabric 48-star American flag attached to a white plastic flagpole with a Lionel pennant flying beneath it. Early version with stitched-edged flags.	30	50	75	4
Later production with edge stitching omitted.	25	40	60	4
90 CONTROLLER: 1955-66, SPST push button normally open momentary contact switch.				
With shiny metal clip retaining a piece of cardstock that could be used to label the switch.	3	8	14	3
Without metal clip.	1	2	10	2
With "No. 90 CONTROL" molded into case.	1	2	10	2
91 CIRCUIT BREAKER: 1957-60, electro-magnetic adjustable circuit breaker.	20	25	30	6
92 CIRCUIT BREAKER CONTROLLER: 1959-69, looks like a 90 Controller.				
Packed in a manila envelope.	5	10	15	4
Packed in a traditional box.	5	10	15	4
Carded blister pack, 1966.	-	90	175	7
93 WATER TOWER: Prewar and 1946-49. Postwar versions, like some prewar, are silver.	25	40	70	4
96C CONTROLLER: 1938-1942, 1945-54, SPST push button normally open momentary contact switch.	1	2	5	2
97 COAL ELEVATOR: 1938-1942, 1946-1950. All years except 1942 have silver supporting structure.	100	175	225	5
108 TRESTLE SET: 1959, set of 12 unpainted black plastic trestle piers (two each lettered A-F) packaged in overstamped 1044 transformer boxes. The value here is entirely in the box.	30	45	100	6
109 TRESTLE SET: 1961, set of 12 gray plastic piers was packaged by adhering them to two strips of waxy cardboard.	Too rarely traded to establish accurate pricing.			
110 TRESTLE SET: 1955-69, set of 24 or 22 piers with metal hardware for attaching track.	18	22	35	2
111 TRESTLE SET: 1956-69, set of 10 "A" (the tallest) piers.	15	25	35	4
111-100 TRESTLE PIERS: 1960-63, two gray 4-3/4-inch "A" piers packaged in a 111-10 manila envelope along with the necessary mounting hardware. The value of this item is entirely in the packaging.	40	65	100	7

128 Animated Newsstand

132 Illuminated Station with Automatic Train Control

138 Water Tank

145 Automatic Gateman

	VG	EX	LN	RARITY
112 SUPER 0 SWITCHES: 1957 only, pair of Super 0 remote control non-derailing switches with 022C controllers. The wheel flanges depressing contacting springs mounted in the turnout base controlled the non-derailing feature of these switches.	55	90	100	5
112R SUPER 0 SWITCHES: 1958-66, pair of Super 0 remote control switches. The non-derailing contacts were designed to be operated by the backs of passing wheels.	65	100	125	3
112-125 SUPER 0 SWITCH: 1957-61, single left-hand remote control Super 0 turnout with 022C controller.	40	60	80	5
112-150 SUPER 0 SWITCH: 1957-61, single right-hand remote control Super 0 turnout with 022C controller.	40	60	80	5
112LH SUPER 0 SWITCH: 1962-66, separate sale left-hand Super 0 remote control turnout with 022C controller.	40	60	80	5
112RH SUPER 0 SWITCH: 1962-66, separate sale right-hand Super 0 remote control turnout with 022C controller.	40	60	80	5
114 NEWSSTAND WITH HORN: 1957-59, newsstand with battery-operated horn.	75	115	150	4
115 LIONEL CITY STATION: 1935-42, 1946-49.	250	350	550	5
118 NEWSSTAND WITH WHISTLE: 1957-58.	60	100	125	4
119 LANDSCAPED TUNNEL: 1957-58, 14 inches long, 10 inches wide, eight inches high vacuum-formed plastic tunnel.	Too infrequently offered in Lionel packaging to establish value.			
120 90-DEGREE CROSSING: 1957-66, 90-degree Super 0 crossing.	5	10	15	4
121 LANDSCAPED TUNNEL: 1959-66, Styrofoam tunnel made by Life-Like products and sold by Lionel. Lionel packaging is essential to its value as a Lionel collectable.	Too infrequently offered in Lionel packaging to establish value.			
122 LAMP ASSORTMENT: 1948-49, assortment of individually boxed bulbs.	200	325	600	7
1950-52, the bulbs pressed into a paperboard insert.	150	250	475	7
123 LAMP ASSORTMENT: 1953-59, bulbs pressed into a paperboard insert.	150	250	450	7
123-60 LAMP ASSORTMENT: 1960-63, assortment used a different style box, which in turn held 12 boxes of 10 lamps.	200	300	500	7
125 WHISTLE SHACK: 1950-55, dark gray plastic base with either red or maroon roof.	25	45	60	4
Bright green base with maroon roof.	30	55	70	5

148 Dwarf Signal

150 Telegraph Pole Set

152 Automatic Crossing Gate

151 Semphore

	VG	EX	LN	RARITY
Dark green base with maroon roof.	30	55	70	5
Light gray base with maroon roof.	25	45	60	4
128 ANIMATED NEWSSTAND: 1957-60.	125	175	225	4
130 60-DEGREE CROSSING: 1957-66, 60-degree crossing for Super 0.	10	14	18	6
131 CURVED TUNNEL: 1957-66, Styrofoam tunnel made by Life-Like products, the Lionel packaging is essential to its value as a Lionel collectible.	Too infrequently offered in Lionel packaging to establish value.			
132 ILLUMINATED STATION WITH AUTOMATIC TRAIN CONTROL: 1949-55.	75	110	150	3
133 ILLUMINATED PASSENGER STATION: 1957, 1961-62 and 1966.	50	75	100	3
138 WATER TANK: 1953, unpainted gray plastic roof.	125	175	200	5
1954-57, unpainted bright orange plastic.	100	150	175	3

140 AUTOMATIC BANJO SIGNAL: 1954-66, with 145C contactor.

	VG	EX	LN	RARITY
Packed in a box.	30	40	55	4
Blister packed to a card.	-	150	275	7
142 MANUAL SWITCHES: 1957-66, pair of manually operated Super 0 turnouts.	30	40	55	4
142-125 SUPER 0 SWITCH: 1957-61, single left-hand Super 0 manually operated turnout.	20	30	40	5
142-150 SUPER 0 SWITCH: 1957-61, single right-hand Super 0 manually operated turnout.	20	30	40	5
142LH SUPER 0 SWITCH: 1962, single left-hand Super 0 manually operated turnout.	20	30	40	5
142RH SUPER 0 SWITCH: 1962, single right-hand Super 0 manually operated turnout.	20	30	40	5
145 AUTOMATIC GATEMAN: 1950-66.	30	40	55	2
145C CONTACTOR: 1950-60, SPST pressure-activated normally open momentary contact switch.	1	2	10	1
147 WHISTLE CONTROLLER: 1961-66, controller contained a D-cell battery and a fast-acting switch.	2	4	10	2

154 Automatic Highway Signal

155 Bell Ringing Signal

156 Illuminated Station Platform

164 Log Loader

	VG	EX	LN	RARITY
148 DWARF SIGNAL: 1957-60, furnished with 148C switch, which was a DPDT version of the common SPST 364C. Without the controller, the accessory is not complete.	50	65	125	6
150 TELEGRAPH POLE SET: 1947-50. Set of six brown plastic poles with metal base clips used to attach the poles to the track ties.	40	60	80	5
151 SEMAPHORE: 1947-69. Green base, arrow on the semaphore arm raised, bulk of blade painted yellow.	50	85	110	6
Black base, arrow on the semaphore arm raised and painted yellow.	20	28	40	3
Black base, arrow on the semaphore arm raised and painted red.	80	125	200	7
Black base, arrow on the semaphore arm recessed and painted yellow.	20	28	40	3
Packed in carded blister pack.	-	190	300	7
152 AUTOMATIC CROSSING GATE: 1945-49, prewar, all postwar produced accessories have their gates painted silver.	20	40	60	5
152-33 12-VOLT RED LAMPS: Replacement lamp individually packed in its own tiny orange and blue "Lionel Trains" box for retail sale. Twelve boxes were packed into a larger orange and blue box for dealer sales. The values listed below are for individual bulbs. When a 12-pack box, as shown, is offered the value of the 12-pack is 100 times the value of the individual bulb.	3	4	5	6
153 AUTOMATIC BLOCK SIGNAL AND CONTROL: 1940-42, 1945-59, furnished with a 153C contactor.	30	40	55	3
153-23 6-8-VOLT RED LAMPS: Replacement lamp individually packed in its own tiny orange and blue "Lionel Trains" box for retail sale. Twelve boxes were packed into a larger orange and blue box for dealer sales. The values listed below are for individual bulbs. When a 12-pack box, as shown, is offered the value of the 12-pack is 100 times the value of the individual bulb.	3	4	5	6
153C CONTACTOR: 1945-69, single pole, double throw pressure-activated momentary contact switch for use actuating signals.	1	2	10	1

153-50 14-Volt Red Lamps

154-18 12-Volt Red Lamps

157 Illuminated Station Platform

163 Single Target Block Signal

	VG	EX	LN	RARITY
153-50 14-VOLT RED LAMPS: Replacement lamp individually packed in its own tiny orange and blue "Lionel Trains" box for retail sale. Twelve boxes were packed into a larger orange and blue box for dealer sales. The values listed below are for individual bulbs. When a 12-pack box, as shown, is offered the value of the 12-pack is 100 times the value of the individual bulb.	3	4	5	6
154 AUTOMATIC HIGHWAY SIGNAL: 1946-69, two red-painted screw-base bulbs, white die-cast crossbuck.	30	40	55	3
1950-69, red bayonet-based bulbs, white plastic crossbuck.	30	40	55	3
1966, in carded blister pack.	-	150	300	7
154-18 12-VOLT RED LAMPS: Replacement lamp individually packed in its own tiny orange and blue "Lionel Trains" box for retail sale. Twelve boxes were packed into a larger orange and blue box for dealer sales. The values listed below are for individual bulbs. When a 12-pack box, as shown, is offered the value of the 12-pack is 100 times the value of the individual bulb.	3	4	5	6
155 BELL RINGING SIGNAL: 1955-57.				
1955 signals did not have "feet," and copper blade-type contacts were used on the mechanism.	45	60	75	4
1956-57 production signals had plastic feet molded into the base and redesigned spring-type contacts.	45	60	75	4
156 ILLUMINATED STATION PLATFORM: 1939-42, 1946-51.	60	85	150	4
157 ILLUMINATED STATION PLATFORM: 1952-59, red plastic base and a dark green roof.	40	65	85	5
Maroon plastic base and a medium green roof.	30	45	60	4
161 MAIL PICKUP SET: 1961-1963.	65	100	150	6
163 SINGLE TARGET BLOCK SIGNAL: 1961-69, boxed.	30	40	55	3
Blister packed.	-	225	350	7
164 LOG LOADER: 1940-42, 1946-50.	150	225	400	4
167 WHISTLE CONTROLLER: 1946-57.	4	8	15	1

182 Triple Action Magnet Crane

193 Industrial Water Tower

197 Rotating Radar Antenna

214 Plate Girdes Bridge

	VG	EX	LN	RARITY
175 ROCKET LAUNCHER: 1958-60.	125	250	475	6
175-50 EXTRA ROCKET: 1959-60. Prices shown are for a six-pack.	150	225	475	8
182 TRIPLE ACTION MAGNET CRANE: 1946-49, clear-molded smokestack painted gray.	150	250	350	5
Smokestacks painted black.	150	250	350	5
192 OPERATING CONTROL TOWER: 1959-60.	150	200	275	5
193 INDUSTRIAL WATER TOWER: 1953-55, sheet metal supporting structure painted black.	100	150	225	7
Red-painted supporting structure.	85	115	175	4
195 FLOODLIGHT TOWER: 1957-69.	45	60	75	3
Molded-in legend "199 MICROWAVE TOWER" but rubber stamped "195 FLOOD LIGHT" in red.	60	75	100	6
195-75 EIGHT-BULB FLOODLIGHT EXTENSION: 1957-60, this was a standard eight-bulb array from a 195 floodlight tower, plus two extension posts.	20	35	75	5
196 SMOKE PELLETS: 1946-47, small clear plastic box, sealed with a wire bail.	40	75	125	7
197 ROTATING RADAR ANTENNA: 1957-59, with orange platform structure.	100	125	225	5
With gray platform structure.	80	100	175	3
197-75 RADAR HEAD: 1957-60, the package is critical to the value of this item.	100	150	250	6
199 MICROWAVE RELAY TOWER: 1958-59, black base and platform with a gray tower.	40	75	145	5
206 ARTIFICIAL COAL: 1946-59, half-pound cloth bags filled with ground Bakelite "coal" lettered with red "No. 206" "ARTIFICIAL COAL" and Lionel markings.	5	10	18	3
214 PLATE GIRDER BRIDGE: 1953-69. Raised white "LIONEL" lettering along the side.	15	20	30	3
Without white highlighting on the lettering.	15	20	30	3
Raised "U. S. STEEL" highlighted in white.	20	25	50	3
Raised "U.S. STEEL" and "6418" highlighted in white.	20	25	50	3
Carded and blister packed.	-	300	550	7

256 Freight Station

264 Operating Forklift

282 Portal Gantry Crane

299 Code Transmitter Set

	VG	EX	LN	RARITY
252 CROSSING GATE: 1950-63.	25	30	50	2
253 AUTOMATIC BLOCK SIGNAL: 1956-59, tan plastic base with the simulated relay box portion painted black.	30	45	70	6
Unpainted tan plastic base.	20	30	50	4
256 FREIGHT STATION: 1950-53, dark green roof.	40	60	90	4
Light, bright green roof molding.	75	125	210	6
257 FREIGHT STATION WITH DIESEL HORN: 1956-57, dark green roof and a maroon base.	60	75	125	4
Lighter, brighter green roof molding.	75	125	210	6
Dark green roof and brown base.	80	100	145	4
260 BUMPER: 1951-69.				
1951-57, red die-cast housing, copper center rail contact with inverted V-shaped notch.	15	20	25	3
1958-65, red die-cast housing, no inverted V-shape notch in the power contact.	15	20	25	3
1966, unpainted black plastic housing, packaged in carded blister pack.	-	200	300	7
1968-69, unpainted black plastic housing, non-illuminated, packed in a box.	30	40	50	5
262 HIGHWAY CROSSING GATE: 1962-69. Packed in box.	50	75	100	4
1966, packed in blister packaging.	-	100	175	6
264 OPERATING FORKLIFT: 1957-60, came with 6264 flatcar.	250	325	450	6
282 PORTAL GANTRY CRANE: 1954-55.	140	190	275	6
282R GANTRY CRANE: 1956-57.	140	190	275	6
299 CODE TRANSMITTER SET: 1961-63, packed with the tower was a 299-25 telegraph key.	100	125	175	6
308 RAILROAD SIGN SET: 1940-42, 1945-49. The set included five different die-cast signposts.	35	50	90	5
309 YARD SIGN SET: 1950-59, nine plastic signs with die-cast metal bases.	20	30	55	4

313 Bascule Bridge

342 Culvert Loader

345 Culvert Unloading Station

346 Operating Culvert Unloader

	VG	EX	LN	RARITY
310 BILLBOARD: 1950-68. Five unpainted green plastic billboard frames, with perforated die-cut sheets of cardboard billboards. Many different products were promoted, and some are quite hard to find. The values listed below are for the common versions. Like New value assumes all the cardboard signs are present and have not been separated.	5	10	40	1

313 BASCULE BRIDGE: 1940-42, 1946-49. The prewar version is distinguished by having a square gearbox inside the support tower nearest the bridge tender's house. In the postwar version, the gearbox was L-shaped.

	VG	EX	LN	RARITY
1946-47, smooth-topped red R-68 warning lamp lens.	300	525	675	5
1948-49, ribbed-topped red RW-27 warning lamp lens.	300	525	675	5
313-82 FIBER PINS: 1946-60, one dozen 027 insulating pins. The collector value of this item is in the packaging.	1	2	3	2
313-121 FIBER PINS: 1961, one dozen 027 insulating pins. The collector value of this item is in the packaging.	1	2	3	2

314 PLATE GIRDER BRIDGE: 1940-42, 1945-50, die-cast, painted gray during the postwar era.

	VG	EX	LN	RARITY
1945-1946, painted dark gray with 11/32-inch tall "LIONEL" lettering.	25	35	50	3
1947-50, painted light gray with 3/8-inch tall "LIONEL" lettering.	25	35	50	3
315 ILLUMINATED TRESTLE BRIDGE: 1940-42, 1946-47. Painted silver every year but 1942.	75	100	125	5
316 TRESTLE BRIDGE: 1941-42, 1949. Lionel nomenclature and stock number embossed in the bottom plate postwar, whereas this information was rubber stamped on the prewar version.	25	40	55	4
317 TRESTLE BRIDGE: 1950-56, was identical to the 316 except for the embossed number and gray instead of silver paint.	25	35	50	3
321 TRESTLE BRIDGE: 1958-64, sheet metal base and unpainted gray plastic sides and top. Shipped unassembled.	20	35	50	3
332 ARCH UNDER BRIDGE: 1959-66.	30	45	60	4
334 DISPATCHING BOARD: 1957-60.	175	250	350	5
342 CULVERT LOADER: 1956-58.	150	225	400	5
345 CULVERT UNLOADING STATION: 1957-59.	150	300	500	6
346 OPERATING CULVERT UNLOADER: 1965-66, hand-operated version of the 345.	100	150	250	6

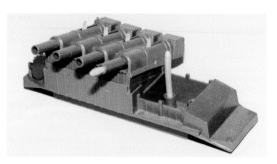

347 Cannon Firing
Range Set

350 Engine Transfer Table

352 Ice Depot

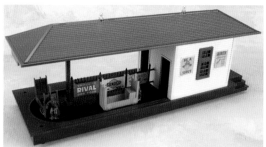

356 Operating
Freight Station

	VG	EX	LN	RARITY
347 CANNON FIRING RANGE SET: 1964.	200	600	1,200	8
348 OPERATING CULVERT UNLOADER: 1966-69, a 346 with a paper label reading "348" was pasted over 346 on the box, and the inner packaging was changed to accommodate the 6342 gondola car.	125	175	275	6
350 ENGINE TRANSFER TABLE: 1957-60.	150	325	500	5
350-50 TRANSFER TABLE EXTENSION: 1957-60.	125	175	250	6
352 ICE DEPOT: 1955-57. Unpainted brown plastic platform, furnished with a car that had four lines of rubber-stamped data on the ice compartment door.	175	275	350	5
Unpainted red plastic platform, furnished with a car that had four lines of rubber-stamped data on the ice compartment door.	175	250	375	4
Unpainted red plastic platform, furnished with a car that had three lines of heat-stamped lettering on the ice compartment door.	225	325	475	6
353 TRACK SIDE CONTROL SIGNAL: 1960-61, furnished with 153C contactor.	20	30	45	5
356 OPERATING FREIGHT STATION: 1952-57, as originally produced in 1952, station had a dark green roof. Dark green and orange baggage carts. It also came with a colorful lithographed tin insert for one of the baggage carts representing a load of luggage.	150	185	250	7
1952-57, station as above, only without the lithographed loads.	60	90	140	4
One tomato red baggage cart and one light green baggage cart.	125	160	220	6
Roof molded in the same light green colored plastic used for the 497 roof.	90	125	175	5
362 BARREL LOADER: 1952-57, with a box of six brown-stained wooden barrels, 364C controller, rubber track spacers, and later editions also included a metal platform extension and metal track spacing guides.				
Large white rubber man, "LIONEL" sign highlighted in red. Metal base plate cadmium plated.	150	200	325	7
Large white rubber man, "LIONEL" sign highlighted in gold. Metal base plate cadmium plated.	90	125	175	5
Large blue rubber man with painted face and hands, "LIONEL" sign highlighted in gold. Metal base plate cadmium plated.	70	100	150	4
Large unpainted blue rubber man, "LIONEL" sign highlighted in gold. Metal base plate painted black.	70	100	150	4

364 Lumber Loader

394 Rotating Beacon

397 Operating Coal Loader

419 Heliport

	VG	EX	LN	RARITY
362-78 BARRELS: 1952-57, small box containing six brown-stained small wooden barrels.	5	10	25	3
364 LUMBER LOADER: 1948-57, dark crackle gray finish.	100	150	200	5
Light gray hammer tone finish.	90	125	175	4
364C ON-OFF SWITCH: 1959-64, off-on slide switch.	2	8	16	5
365 DISPATCHING STATION: 1958-59, molded-in number on the base reads "365."	80	115	140	4
375 TURNTABLE: 1962-64.	125	175	225	5
390C SWITCH: 1960-64, double pole, double throw switch for use on HO layouts.	5	10	20	7
394 ROTATING BEACON: 1949-53, painted red.	30	40	55	3
Painted dark green.	50	75	100	5
Made of unpainted aluminum.	20	30	45	3
Red steel base with unpainted aluminum tower and platform.	30	40	55	4
395 FLOODLIGHT TOWER: 1949-56, silver-painted steel structure.	25	40	60	3
Green-painted steel tower.	25	40	60	3
Unpainted aluminum.	30	45	70	4
Red-painted steel tower.	30	50	75	4
Yellow-painted steel tower.	100	140	200	6
397 OPERATING COAL LOADER: 1948-57. Came with a bag of coal, a 364C on-off switch and the requisite hook-up wire and instruction sheets.				
Yellow-painted GM motor housing and a number 70 Yard Light.	250	350	550	7
Blue-painted GM motor housing.	125	175	225	4
410 BILLBOARD BLINKER: 1956-58.	30	50	85	5
413 COUNTDOWN CONTROL PANEL: 1962 only.	45	75	125	5
415 DIESEL FUELING STATION: 1955-67.	100	145	200	5
419 HELIPORT: 1962, included a yellow helicopter.	175	425	725	6

445 Operating Switch Tower

455 Operating Oil Derrick

460 Piggy Back Transportation Set

460-150 Two Trailers

	VG	EX	LN	RARITY
443 MISSILE LAUNCHING PLATFORM WITH EXPLODING AMMUNITION DUMP: 1960-62.	25	40	80	4
445 OPERATING SWITCH TOWER: 1952-57.	40	75	100	3
448 MISSILE FIRING RANGE SET: 1961-63.	90	200	300	5
450 SIGNAL BRIDGE: 1952-58, furnished with a single 153C controller.	50	65	100	4
450L SIGNAL BRIDGE HEAD: 1952-58, small Traditional box containing a blackened die-cast twin lamp socket with bulbs and a black hood.	40	60	125	6
452 GANTRY SIGNAL BRIDGE: 1961-63, furnished with a 153C contactor.	75	110	175	6
455 OPERATING OIL DERRICK: 1950-54, dark green tower with a red platform near its top.	200	275	375	4
Dark green tower with matching upper platform.	175	225	300	4
Pale green tower.	300	450	600	7
456 COAL RAMP: 1950-55, supplied with a special 456-100 controller, a 3456 operating hopper car, 456-83 maroon plastic receiving bin, two 456-85 coal pin mounting posts, a 456-84 coal bin door and a bag of 206 coal.				
Dark gray with handrails made of braided steel wire.	200	275	350	6
Dark gray with handrails made of fishing line.	175	225	300	6
Light gray with handrails made of fishing line.	150	200	275	5
460 PIGGY BACK TRANSPORTATION SET: 1955-57, furnished with two green plastic "LIONEL TRAINS" trailers with "FRUEHAUF" and "DURAVAN" signs on the front.				
Forklift with small, self-adhesive sign affixed to each side, which read "ROSS TRAILOADER."	100	150	200	4
Forklift with rubber-stamped "ROSS TRAILOADER" markings.	125	175	250	5
460P PIGGY BACK PLATFORM: This is the platform only from the 460 set, without the trailers or flatcar. The box must be present in order for this to have any real value.	300	550	850	6
460-150 TWO TRAILERS: 1955-57, box labeled "No. 460-150/TWO TRAILERS."	100	250	475	6
461 PLATFORM WITH TRUCK AND TRAILER: 1966, lacks the depressions molded into the top of the 460 to receive the trailer wheels. The forklift lacks "Ross Trailoader" markings. Came with a white single axle Lionel-made trailer and a red die-cast tractor made by Midge and marked "MIDGE TOY, ROCKFORD. ILL. U.S.A. PATENT 2775847."	100	150	250	6

462 Derrick Platform Set

464 Lumber Mill

465 Sound Dispatching
Station

497 Coaling
Station

	VG	EX	LN	RARITY
462 DERRICK PLATFORM SET: 1961-62.	200	250	325	6
464 LUMBER MILL: 1956-60, with a 364C controller, logs and lumber.	125	175	225	4
465 SOUND DISPATCHING STATION: 1956-57, with a gray plastic microphone equipped.	100	140	175	4
470 MISSILE LAUNCHING PLATFORM WITH EXPLODING TARGET CAR: 1959-62, exploding 6470 target car with a red and white missile.	100	150	210	3
494 ROTARY BEACON: 1954-66, produced in red-painted steel, silver-painted steel and in unpainted aluminum. All are equally desirable and common.	30	40	50	3
497 COALING STATION: 1953-58, dark green roof with small mounting tabs.	150	200	300	5
Light green roof with large mounting tabs.	125	160	230	4
Dark green roof with large mounting tabs.	150	175	250	5
671-75 SPECIAL SMOKE BULB: Replacement for special bulb used in 1946's 671 and 2020 locomotives.	10	20	30	5
703-10 SPECIAL SMOKE BULB: Replacement for special bulb used in 1946's 726 locomotives.	15	30	55	6
760 072 TRACK: 1938-42, 1950, 1954-58, box of 16 sections of 072 curved track. The prices below are predicated on the presence of the original box.	50	75	145	5
902 ELEVATED TRESTLE SET: 1959-60, component of uncataloged sets, packaged in a paper sack labeled "902 ELEVATED TRESTLE SET." Included were 10 trestles, 10 railroad signs, a girder bridge and a tunnel, all punch-out cardboard construction. Prices include bag and un-punched cardboard sheets.	-	125	300	8
908 RAILROAD TERMINAL: 1964.	-	-	-	8
909 SMOKE FLUID: 1957-68, bottle contained two ounces of smoke fluid, 12-pack.	25	40	100	4
1966, carded.	30	120	325	8
910 U. S. NAVY SUBMARINE BASE: 1961, made entirely of cardboard.	Too rarely traded to establish accurate pricing.			
919 ARTIFICIAL GRASS: 1946-64, half-pound bags of green-dyed sawdust, sold in white cloth drawstring closure bags, typically with red lettering on the bag.	7	7	30	2

920 Scenic Display Set

928 Maintenance and Lubricant Kit

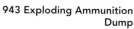

943 Exploding Ammunition Dump

	VG	EX	LN	RARITY
920 SCENIC DISPLAY SET: 1957-58, included a three by four-foot sheet of special felt mountain cloth and two gray plastic tunnel portals. "HILLSIDE" was molded at the top of the portal and a Lionel "L" in circle and "1957" were molded in the base. Also included in the set were bags of 920-5 artificial rock, 920-8 dyed lichen, 920-6 glue, 920-3 green grass, and 920-4 yellow grass. A pallet of watercolor paints was also included, as were a dozen 920-11 steel clips for use attaching the felt to the portals.	40	100	175	6
920-2 TUNNEL PORTALS: 1958-59, set of two gray plastic tunnel portals. "HILLSIDE" was molded at the top of each portal and a Lionel "L" in circle was molded in the portal's left base and "1957" in the right base.	20	35	60	5
920-3 GREEN GRASS: 1957-58, bag of green-dyed sawdust "grass" in a clear plastic bag was printed: **"GREEN GRASS FOR MODEL TRAIN LAYOUTS L THE LIONEL CORPORATION NEW YORK N.Y. Made in U.S. of America 920-17."**	2	10	60	6
920-3 GREEN GRASS: 1957-58, bag of yellow-dyed sawdust "grass" in a clear plastic bag was printed: **"YELLOW GRASS FOR MODEL TRAIN LAYOUTS L THE LIONEL CORPORATION NEW YORK N.Y. Made in U.S. of America 920-18."**	2	10	60	6
920-5 ARTIFICIAL ROCK: 1957-1958, artificial rock made of expanded vermiculite.	5	30	60	7
920-8 LICHEN: 1958, while the product was the same, the packaging was different from that of the more desirable 971 Lichen.	5	25	60	7
927 LUBRICATING AND MAINTENANCE KIT: 1950-59, contains a tube of lubricant, vial of lubricating oil, can of track-cleaning solvent, cleaning sticks, etc. for consumer use cleaning and maintaining their trains.	10	30	70	3
928 MAINTENANCE AND LUBRICANT KIT: 1960-63, included oil, a tube of grease, "Track Clean" solvent and a rubber track-cleaning eraser.	20	40	85	5
943 EXPLODING AMMUNITION DUMP: 1959-61.	30	60	100	4
950 U.S. RAILROAD MAP: 1958-66, 52 x 37-inch map printed by Rand McNally: Prices shown for rolled version, in tube.	60	90	150	4

952 Figure Set

953 Figure Set

963 Frontier Set

963-100 Frontier Set

	VG	EX	LN	RARITY

A note on Lionel Plasticville: The piece count on the packages was a bit odd. A structure, be it five parts or 50 was one "piece," but then so was every chicken, fireplug or tree. In all cases, the true value lies entirely in the Lionel packaging.

	VG	EX	LN	RARITY
951 FARM SET: 1958, 13 pieces including a truck, tractor, jeep, horses, cows, harrow, plow, wagon, and footbridge.	125	200	475	7
952 FIGURE SET: 1958, contains 30 pieces: people, fireplug, fire alarm box and mailboxes.	125	200	475	7
953 FIGURE SET: 1959-62, included 32 pieces and a paintbrush.	125	200	475	7
954 SWIMMING POOL AND PLAYGROUND SET: 1959, included 30 pieces: 12 fence pieces, six trees, slide, swing, teeter-totter, merry-go-round, bench, table with umbrella, two chairs, two chaise lounges, pool.	125	200	475	7
955 HIGHWAY SET: 1958, includes 22 pieces in the box: two buses, auto, seven telegraph poles, 10 yellow street signs, seven green street indicators.	125	200	475	7
956 STOCKYARD SET: 1959, includes corral, as well as cows and railroad signs.	125	200	475	7
957 FARM BUILDING AND ANIMAL SET: 1958, includes 35 pieces, among them four farm buildings, a pump, fence with gate, horse, fowl and domestic animals.	125	200	475	7
958 VEHICLE SET: 1958, three autos, two fire trucks, an ambulance, a bus, various street signs, fire alarm box, mailbox, fireplug, traffic light made of the 24 pieces in this set.	150	275	550	7
959 BARN SET: 1958, 23 pieces: dairy barn, horses, fowl and domestic animals; orange and blue traditional box.	150	275	550	7
960 BARNYARD SET: 1959-61, 29 pieces including three farm buildings, a tractor, truck, wagon, dog house, fowl, domestic, and farm animals.	125	200	475	7
961 SCHOOL SET: 1959, contained 36 pieces, including a school building, a flagpole, two buses, street signs, fence pieces, shrubs, and benches.	125	200	475	7
962 TURNPIKE SET: 1958, 24 pieces, four Bachmann automobiles, an ambulance, a bus, an interchange, stanchions, five telegraph poles, bus, and street signs.	175	300	600	8
963 FRONTIER SET: 1959-60, this set contained 18 pieces: cabin, windmill, fences, cows, and pump.	150	275	550	7
963-100 FRONTIER SET: Contains 18 pieces: cabin, windmill, fences, cows, and pump.	300	500	850	7

971 Lichen

972 Landscape Tree Assortment

973 Complete Landscaping Set

974 Scenery Set

	VG	EX	LN	RARITY
964 FACTORY SITE SET: 1959, 18-piece set included a factory with water tower, four telegraph poles, railroad signs and a Bachmann automobile.	150	275	550	7
965 FARM SET: 1959, 36-piece set including a dairy barn, three smaller farm buildings, and various farm equipment and assorted creatures.	125	200	475	7
966 FIRE HOUSE SET: 1958, 45-piece set included red-roofed white firehouse, two fire engines, an ambulance, an alarm box, Bachmann automobiles, a fire hydrant, bus, traffic light, street signs, street post, bench, mailbox, people, telegraph poles, and pine trees.	125	200	475	7
967 POST OFFICE SET: 1958, 25 pieces, including post office, mailbox, traffic lights, people, benches, streetlights, street signs, truck, and autos.	125	200	475	7
968 TV TRANSMITTER SET: 1958, 28-piece set including a TV station, Jeep, two Bachmann automobiles, a fence with a gate, people, mailbox, fireplug, and trees.	150	275	550	7
969 CONSTRUCTION SET: 1960, 23 pieces including a house under construction, workmen, construction materials and Bachmann autos.	150	275	550	7
970 TICKET BOOTH: 1958-60, 46 inches tall, 22 inches wide, and 11 inches deep cardboard ticket booth.	-	125	200	6
971 LICHEN: 1960-64, manufactured and packaged by Life-Like products, but were packaged in Lionel boxes and sold by Lionel.	75	175	350	8
972 LANDSCAPE TREE ASSORTMENT: 1961-64, package of four evergreen trees, three flowering shrubs and lichen.	150	325	600	8
973 COMPLETE LANDSCAPING SET: 1960-64, this set included 4 x 8-inch roll of grass mat, one 16 x 48-inch roll each of earth, ballast and road material.	300	1,000	1,500	7
974 SCENERY SET: 1962-63, contains 4 x 8-inch grass mat, two Styrofoam 3-D background mountains, a bag of lichen, and nine assorted trees.	700	2,500	4,000	8
980 RANCH SET: 1960, 14-piece set includes a loading pen, cattle, pigs, sheep, and farm implements.	125	225	475	7
981 FREIGHT YARD SET: 1960, contains 10 pieces including a loading platform and associated parts, a switch tower, telephone poles, and figures.	125	225	475	7

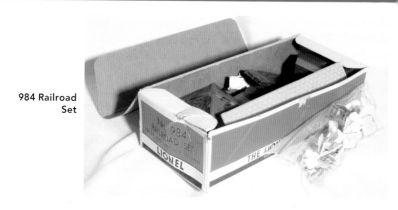

984 Railroad
Set

987 Town Set

1008 Uncoupling Unit

1011
Transformer

	VG	EX	LN	RARITY
982 SUBURBAN SPLIT LEVEL SET: 1960, 18-piece set, centered around a split level house, and included pine trees, an automobile, and a fence.	125	225	475	7
983 FARM SET: 1960-61, set included seven pieces; a dairy barn, Colonial house, automobile, horse, cows, and windmill.	125	225	475	7
984 RAILROAD SET: 1961-62, contains 22 pieces, including a switch tower, loading platform, figures, R.R. signs, and accessories.	125	225	475	7
985 FREIGHT AREA SET: 1961, the 32 pieces included were a water tower, a work car converted to storage shed, a loading platform, a switch tower, a watchman's shanty, automobiles, telegraph poles, R.R. signs, and accessories.	125	225	475	7
986 FARM SET: 1962, 20-piece farm set featuring a farmhouse, a barn and 18 domestic animals.	125	225	475	7
987 TOWN SET: 1962, 24 pieces including a church, a combination bank and store, a gas station with pumps, a Bachmann automobile, 12 street signs, and five telegraph poles.	400	750	1,250	8
988 RAILROAD STRUCTURE SET: 1962, 16-piece set including a railroad station with freight platform, a water tank, hobo shacks, a shanty, a storage shed made from a railroad car, a bench, figures, and a crossing gate.	150	300	550	8
1008 UNCOUPLING UNIT: 1957-62, also known as Cam-Trol uncoupler.	1	2	5	1
1008-50 UNCOUPLING TRACK SECTION: 1957-62.	1	2	5	1
1009 MANUMATIC UNCOUPLER: 1948-52.	1	2	5	1
1010 TRANSFORMER: 1961-66, 35-watt, 110-volt primary transformer with speed and direction controls.	10	20	25	2
1011 TRANSFORMER: 1948-52, 25-watt, 110-volt primary transformer with speed control and circuit breaker.	10	15	20	2
1011X TRANSFORMER: 1948-52, 25-watt, 125-volt, 25-cycle current.	10	15	20	2
1012 TRANSFORMER: 1950-54, 35-watt, 110-volt primary transformer with speed control and circuit breaker.	20	30	40	5
1013 CURVED TRACK: Sold throughout the duration of the postwar era, 027 curved track is easily the most common single item Lionel produced. The crossties came in black, gray and brown depending upon era. The only variation of this with any real value is the 1966 blister-packaged four-pack listed here.	20	30	50	5

1018 Straight Track

1019 Remote Control Track Set

1020 90-Degree Crossing

1022 LH & RH Manual Switch

	VG	EX	LN	RARITY
1013-17 STEEL PINS: 1946-60, 12-pack of steel track pins for 027-Gauge track. The value here is in the sealed original package.	-	.50	1	1
1013-42 STEEL PINS: 1961-69, 12-pack of steel track pins for 027-Gauge track. The value here is in the sealed original package.	-	.50	1	1
1014 TRANSFORMER: 1955, 40-watt, 110-volt primary transformer with speed control and circuit breaker.	15	25	40	2
1015 TRANSFORMER: 1956-60, 45-watt, 110-volt primary transformer with speed control and circuit breaker.	25	35	45	2
1016 TRANSFORMER: 1959-60, 35-watt, 110-volt primary transformer with speed control and circuit breaker.				
1959, no directional controls.	10	20	30	2
1960, includes directional controls.	10	20	30	2
1018 STRAIGHT TRACK: Sold throughout the duration of the postwar era, the 8-7/8-inch long sections came with black, gray and brown crossties depending upon era. The only variation of this with any real value is the 1966 blister-packaged four-pack of straight track, whose value is listed here.	25	40	60	5
1019 REMOTE CONTROL TRACK SET: 1946-50, 027 uncoupling track with controller.	5	8	10	3
1020 90-DEGREE CROSSING: 1955-69, plastic-based 027 90-degree crossing. Common boxed version.	2	4	7	3
1966, blister packed version.	-	200	265	7
1021 90-DEGREE CROSSING: 1933-42, 1945-54, steel-based 027 90-degree crossing.	2	4	8	3
1022 MANUAL SWITCHES: 1953-69, a large part of the value listed below is predicated on the presence of the original packaging.	15	20	30	3
1022LH MANUAL SWITCH: 1953-69, a large part of the value listed below is predicated on the presence of the original packaging. Conventional packaging.	8	10	16	3
1966, carded blister pack.	40	50	65	7
1022RH MANUAL SWITCH: 1953-69, a large part of the value listed below is predicated on the presence of the original packaging. Conventional packaging.	8	10	16	3
1966, carded blister pack.	40	50	65	7

1023 45-Degree Crossing

1033 Transformer

1034 Transformer

1043-500 Transformer

	VG	EX	LN	RARITY
1023 45-DEGREE CROSSING: 1956-69, plastic-based 027 crossing. Common boxed version.	3	6	10	3
1966, blister packed version.	-	260	375	7
1024 MANUAL SWITCHES: 1935-42, 1946-52, metal turnouts with circular red and green-painted circular direction markers.	10	20	25	3
1025 ILLUMINATED BUMPER: 1940-42, 1946-47, die-cast black illuminated bumper attached to a section of 027 straight track.	10	15	20	4
1025 TRANSFORMER: 1961-66, 1969, 45-watt, 110-volt primary transformer with speed control and circuit breaker.	25	35	45	2
1026 TRANSFORMER: 1961-64, 25-watt, 110-volt primary transformer with speed control and circuit breaker.	10	15	20	2
1032 TRANSFORMER: 1948 only, 75-watt, 110-volt primary transformer with speed, whistle and direction controls.	20	35	60	3
1032M TRANSFORMER: 1948 only, 75-watt transformer with 125-volt, 50-cycle primary. It was equipped with speed, whistle and direction controls.	30	45	70	7
1033 TRANSFORMER: 1948-56, 90-watt transformer with speed, whistle and direction controls as well as fixed voltage taps.	40	60	90	2
1034 TRANSFORMER: 1948-54, 75-watt, 110-volt primary transformer with speed and direction controls as well as fixed voltage taps.	20	35	60	3
1035 TRANSFORMER: 1947 only, 60-watt, 110-volt primary transformer had a speed control and circuit breaker.	5	10	15	1
1037 TRANSFORMER: 1946-47, 40-watt, 110-volt primary transformer had a speed control and circuit breaker.	10	15	25	3
1041 TRANSFORMER: 1945-46, 60-watt, 110-volt primary transformer with speed, whistle and direction controls.	20	35	50	4
1042 TRANSFORMER: 1947-48, 75-watt, 110-volt primary transformer with built-in speed, direction and whistle controls as well as fixed voltage taps.	25	40	60	4
1043 TRANSFORMER: 1953-58, 50-watt, 110-volt primary transformer with speed control and circuit breaker.	20	35	50	3
1043-500 TRANSFORMER: 1957-58, has ivory-colored case, white cord and gold-colored handle was made especially for inclusion in the 1587S Lady Lionel outfit. Strangely, it was rated at 60 watts, versus the normal 1043's 50-watt rating.	75	125	175	6

1045 Operating Watchman

1047 Operating Switchman

1063 Transformer

1073 Transformer

	VG	EX	LN	RARITY
1043M TRANSFORMER: 1953-58, 50-watt 1043 with a 125-volt, 25-cycle primary. Includes speed control and circuit breaker, but no whistle or directional controls, nor fixed voltage taps.	40	55	75	7
1044 TRANSFORMER: 1957-69, 90-watt, 110-volt primary transformer with built-in speed, direction and whistle controls, as well as fixed voltage taps.	40	65	90	3
1044M TRANSFORMER: 1957-66, made for the Mexican market, this 90-watt, 125-volt, 25-cycle primary transformer had built-in speed, direction and whistle controls, as well as fixed voltage taps.	40	65	90	7
1045 OPERATING WATCHMAN: 1938-42, 1946-50.	20	35	50	4
1047 OPERATING SWITCHMAN: 1959-61.	90	125	170	6
1053 TRANSFORMER: 1956-60, 60-watt, 110-volt primary transformer with built-in speed and whistle controls.	20	35	45	3
1063 TRANSFORMER: 1960-64, 75-watt, 110-volt primary transformer with built-in speed and whistle controls.	25	40	60	3
1063-100 TRANSFORMER: 1961 only, visually identifiable by its green rather than red whistle button, this 75-watt, 110-volt primary transformer had a modified whistle control circuit for use with Scout-type locomotives.	30	45	65	5
1073 TRANSFORMER: 1961-66, 60-watt, 110-volt primary transformer had a speed control and circuit breaker, but no whistle or directional controls, nor fixed voltage taps.	20	30	50	3
1121 REMOTE CONTROL SWITCHES: 1946-51, prewar. Postwar version had plastic rather than metal controller and mechanism covers. Prior to 1950 screw-based lamps were used, later turnouts used bayonet-based bulbs. Early turnouts had flat plastic direction indicator lenses; later ones used a protruding ribbed rubber lens.	20	35	45	3
1122 REMOTE CONTROL SWITCHES: 1952.	17	30	35	4
1122E REMOTE CONTROL SWITCHES: 1953-69, pair of turnouts packaged with 1122-100 controller.	20	35	45	3
1122LH SWITCH: 1955-69, 1122E left-hand 027 turnout was offered for separate sale. When sold this way the turnout was supplied with a 022C controller, although the controller lights will not illuminate when used with a 027 switch.	12	18	25	4

1122RH Switch

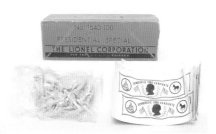

1640-100 Presidential Special

2002 Track Make-Up Kit

3330-100 Operating
Submarine Kit

	VG	EX	LN	RARITY
1122RH SWITCH: 1955-69, 1122E right-hand 027 turnout was offered for separate sale. When sold this way the turnout was supplied with a 022C controller, although the controller lights will not illuminate when used with a 027 switch.	12	18	25	4
1122-234 FIBER PINS: 1958-60, one dozen 027 insulating pins. The collector value of this item is in the packaging.	1	2	3	2
1122-500 027-GAUGE ADAPTER: 1957-66, small envelope of parts necessary to use 027 switches with Super 0 track.	1	2	3	3
1144 TRANSFORMER: 1961-66, 75-watt, 110-volt primary transformer with speed and direction controls.	10	20	40	3
1232 TRANSFORMER: 1948 only, 75-watt, 220-volt primary transformer with speed, whistle and direction controls for use in Europe.	50	100	150	7
1241 TRANSFORMER: 1947-48, 60-watt, 220-volt primary transformer with speed, whistle and direction controls for use in Europe.	50	100	150	7
1244 TRANSFORMER: 1957-66, 90-watt, 220-volt primary transformer with built-in speed, direction and whistle controls, as well as fixed voltage taps for use in Europe.	50	100	150	5
1640-100 PRESIDENTIAL SPECIAL: 1960, includes paper signs for passenger cars indicating Secret Service, Press Corps, and both political parties, and a bag of Plasticville citizens was included to represent a whistle stop audience.	100	250	475	7
2001 TRACK MAKE-UP KIT: 1963 only, common 027 items but the box is extraordinarily rare. This set contained four No. 1013 curved tracks, four No. 1018 straight tracks and one No. 1012 90-degree crossover.	Insufficient sales data to establish pricing.			
2002 TRACK MAKE-UP KIT: 1963 only, common 027 items but the box is extraordinarily rare. This set contained two No. 1013 curved tracks, four No. 1018 straight tracks and one pair No. 1122E remote control switches.	Insufficient sales data to establish pricing.			
2003 TRACK MAKE-UP KIT: 1963 only, common 027 items but the box is extraordinarily rare. This set contained eight No. 1013 curved tracks, two No. 1018 straight tracks and one No. 1023 45-degree crossover.	Insufficient sales data to establish pricing.			
3330-100 OPERATING SUBMARINE KIT: 1960-61.	100	225	350	5
6009 UNCOUPLING SECTION: 1953-55, supplied with a 96C controller.	3	6	10	3
6019 REMOTE CONTROL TRACK: 1948-66.	4	6	10	2

6800-60 Airplane

ECU-1 Electronic Control Unit

KW Transformer

LW Transformer

	VG	EX	LN	RARITY
6029 UNCOUPLING TRACK SET: 1955-63.	3	5	7	2
6149 REMOTE CONTROL UNCOUPLING TRACK: 1964-69.	1	5	7	1
6418 BRIDGE: See 214.				
6650-80 MISSILE: 1959-1960, this was a replacement missile for the 6650, 6823, 443 and 470 packed in a plastic bag.	4	10	20	6
6800-60 AIRPLANE: 1957-58, individually boxed black and yellow airplane.	150	350	450	6
A TRANSFORMER: 1947-48, 90-watt, 110-volt primary transformer had a speed control and circuit breaker, but no whistle or directional controls, nor fixed voltage taps.	20	40	50	3
A220 TRANSFORMER: 1947-48, 90-watt, 220-volt primary transformer had a speed control and circuit breaker, but no whistle or directional controls, nor fixed voltage taps, for European market.	50	70	100	7
AX TRANSFORMER: 1947-48, 90-watt transformer with speed control and circuit breaker was equipped with a 110-volt, 25-hertz primary coil. It had no whistle or directional controls, nor fixed voltage taps.	20	40	50	6
CTC LOCKON: 1947-69.	-	-	1	1
ECU-1 ELECTRONIC CONTROL UNIT: 1946-49, key component of Lionel's Electronic Control Sets, this "transmitter" was not sold separately.	40	75	100	6
KW TRANSFORMER: 1950-65, 190-watt, 110-volt primary transformer with dual built-in speed, direction and whistle controls, as well as numerous fixed voltage taps.	100	150	200	4
LTC LOCKON: 1950-69, illuminated lockon.	2	5	12	3
LW TRANSFORMER: 1955-56, 125-watt, 110-volt primary transformer with built-in speed, direction and whistle controls, as well as various fixed voltage taps.	75	100	125	4
OC CURVED TRACK: 1945-61, O-Gauge curved track from 1945-61.	-	.50	1	1
OC-18 STEEL PINS: 1946-60, envelope of one dozen steel pins for O-Gauge track. The collectable is the envelope, not the pins.	-	-	1	3
OC-51 STEEL PINS: 1961 only, envelope of one dozen steel pins for O-Gauge track.	-	-	1	5
OS STRAIGHT TRACK: 1945-61, 10-inch long O-Gauge straight track.	.50	1	2	1

SW Transformer

SP Smoke Pellets

	VG	EX	LN	RARITY
OTC LOCKON: This special lockon was for use with 3359 and 3562. In its base form, its control rails are the proper height for 027 track, additional clips supplied with the lockon shim the contact height to that required for O-Gauge track.	1	2	4	3
Q TRANSFORMER: 1946 only, 75-watt, 110-volt primary transformer with speed control and circuit breaker, but no whistle or directional controls, nor fixed voltage taps.	20	40	60	6
R TRANSFORMER: 1939-42, 1946-47. This transformer had two independent throttles and numerous fixed voltage taps. Its variable voltage posts went up to 24 volts. It did not have whistle or direction controls.				
1939-42 and 1946 had nameplates giving a 100-watt rating.	50	75	100	4
1947 production of the R was rated at 110-watts.	50	75	100	6
RCS REMOTE CONTROL TRACK: 1938-42, 1946-48, O-Gauge control track with two control rails in addition to the normal three rails. These control rails make contact with the head of a rivet housed in a sliding shoe on operating cars and on coil-coupler trucks. This track does not include the electromagnet needed for the later style magnetic couplers.	5	10	15	3
R220 TRANSFORMER: 1948, this transformer was the same as an R, but was adapted for the European market by the use of a 220-volt primary coil rather than the standard 110-volt US-type coil.	50	100	175	7
RW TRANSFORMER: 1948-54, 110-watt, 110-volt primary transformer with built-in speed, direction and whistle controls, as well as fixed voltage taps.	50	75	100	4
S TRANSFORMER: 1947 only, 80-watt, 110-volt primary transformer had built-in speed, direction and whistle controls.	20	35	60	5
SW TRANSFORMER: 1961-66, 130-watt, 110-volt primary transformer had two built-in speed and direction controls, as well as fixed voltage taps. Strangely, it had a whistle control for only one of the throttles.	60	90	125	4
T011-43 INSULATING PINS: 1962-69, envelope of one dozen O-Gauge insulating pins.	1	2	3	2
SP SMOKE PELLETS: 1948-69, bottle of 50 pills. Numerous variations of bottle, lid and marking exist, some of which are collectable to a limited number of people. The values listed are for useable pills.	10	20	30	2

ST-300 Nut Driver Set

ST-325 Screwdriver Set

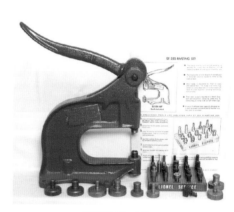

ST-350 Rivet Press

TW Transformer

	VG	EX	LN	RARITY
ST-300 NUT DRIVER SET: As sold by Lionel to their authorized service centers, this set consisted of five nut drivers numbered ST-294 through ST-299 in a blue metal rack. All are marked "LIONEL."	100	150	200	7
ST-302 SPRING ADJUSTING TOOL: This double-ended tool was designed to adjust the tension on flat springs. The different shape of the tool working ends allows repairmen to tweak springs located in difficult to reach locations.	50	75	100	6
ST-325 SCREWDRIVER SET: As sold by Lionel to their authorized service centers, this set consisted of five assorted flat and Phillips head screwdrivers numbered ST-319 through ST-323 in a blue metal ST-324 rack. All are marked "LIONEL," and because of their general utility today it is extremely difficult to find a complete, undamaged set.	180	250	400	8
ST-350 RIVET PRESS: Arguably the most useful of Lionel's service tools was the ST-350 rivet press. Actually manufactured by Chicago Rivet and Machine Co., through the years the ST-350 has been issued in both blue and red. The tooling furnished with these by Chicago Rivet is hardened and has an exceptionally long service life.	400	600	800	5
TOC CURVED TRACK: 1962-66, O-Gauge curved track.	-	.50	1	1
TOC-51 STEEL PINS: 1962-69, envelope of one dozen steel pins for O-Gauge track. The collectible is the envelope, not the pins.	-	-	1	3
TOS STRAIGHT TRACK: 1962-66, 10-inch long O-Gauge straight track.	.50	1	2	1
TW TRANSFORMER: 1953-60, 175-watt, 110-volt primary transformer with whistle, speed and direction controls.				
The 1953 production TW transformers had a terminal labeled "B" on the rear.	75	125	150	4
1954-60 production omitted post "B" from the transformer.	75	125	150	4
T020 90-DEGREE CROSSOVER: 1962-69, 90-degree O-Gauge crossing.	5	7	10	2
T022 REMOTE CONTROL SWITCHES: 1962-69, pair of O-Gauge turnouts with a pair of illuminated 022C controllers.	60	75	110	2
T022-500 O-GAUGE ADAPTER SET: 1962-66, adapters to allow the use of O-Gauge switches with Super 0 track.	2	3	4	4

UCS Remote Control Track

V Transformer

ZW
Transformer

	VG	EX	LN	RARITY
UCS REMOTE CONTROL TRACK: 1949-69, this universal control section could uncouple any O- or 027-Gauge-sized car produced by Lionel as well as actuate any of their electrically triggered operating cars.	8	14	18	2
UTC LOCKON: 1936-42, 1945-46, fits Standard-Gauge track as well as 027, and O-Gauge track.	1	2	4	3
V TRANSFORMER: 1939-41, 1946-47, four-throttle 150-watt transformer with no fixed voltage, direction or whistle controls, but rated at 24 volts.	100	125	150	4
VW TRANSFORMER: 1948-49, four-throttle 150-watt transformer. Shared the distinctive "football in a box" styling with the ZW. These transformers have no fixed voltage connections and direction or whistle controls were provided only for the two outer throttles.	100	125	150	5
Z TRANSFORMER: 1938-42, 1945-47, four-throttle 250-watt transformer with no fixed voltage, direction or whistle controls, but rated at 24 volts.	100	125	150	4
ZW TRANSFORMER: 1948-66, classic four-throttle transformer. It shared the distinctive "football in a box" styling with the VW. These transformers have no fixed voltage connections and direction or whistle controls were provided only for the two outer throttles.				
1948-49, 250 watts, nameplates both on the top and rear.	100	150	225	4
1950-56, 275 watts.	150	200	250	3
1957-66, new designation: ZW(R), although the "R" did not appear on the nameplate.	150	200	250	3

Lionel Cataloged

   While many of us think we got Lionel train sets during the postwar period, a quick look at the period catalogs or boxes will reveal that in most cases we actually received Lionel outfits. Regardless of the terminology, today these outfits, when still with the original individual item boxes and the original outfit carton, are prized collector's items.

   The same components, without the outer outfit carton, are just a group of trains, and lose their outfit or set distinction, and much of the value listed below. In addition to the locomotives and rolling stock shown in these listings, outfits typically came with instruction books and sheets, wire, lockon, accessory catalogs, brochures, smoke pellets and tampers (if applicable), and miniature billboards. All of these items must be present to realize the full value shown. Traditionally, O-Gauge and Super 0 outfits did not include a transformer, which was sold separately, while 027 outfits included a transformer. This situation changed in 1964, when a transformer was supplied with Super 0 outfit 13150. From that point on transformers were supplied with more and more 0 and Super 0 outfits. One item, which normally can be missing from outfits today without affecting the value, is standard 027- and O-Gauge track. Unlike Super 0 track, 0 and 027 track is so common it is almost worthless, and most

Outfits, 1945-1969

collectors feel that the damage caused to the boxes by the track rubbing on it exceeds the value of the track.

Because the value of an outfit is so dependent on the presence and condition of the outfit and component boxes, values are listed for Excellent and Like New examples.

The initial listing is done in numeric order; a chronological listing of cataloged outfit numbers follows the main listing. The outfit number, year, catalog name and the catalog numbers of major components, beginning with locomotive, are shown below.

Please note: Lionel produced many uncataloged outfits as well, some were offered through the normal dealer network, others through mass merchandisers such as Sears and J.C. Penney, and others were used as premiums by firms such as Wix and Swift. These uncataloged outfits, some quite collectable, are not listed here. A final note, a "W" suffix on an outfit number indicates that the train whistled, or had an operating horn; a "B" indicated an operating bell, "S" indicated the locomotive smoked.

463W

1119

1402W

	EX	LN	RARITY
463W: 1945 O-GAUGE FOUR-CAR FREIGHT SET: 224, 2466W, 2458, 2452, 2555, and 2457.	850	1,550	8
1000W: 1955 027 THREE-CAR SET: 2016, 6026W, 6014 red, 6012, and 6017.	200	350	4
1001: 1955 027 THREE-CAR SET: 610, 6012, 6014 red and 6017.	250	475	4
1105: 1959 ADVANCE CATALOG, FOUR-CAR DIESEL FREIGHT: 1055, 6045, 6044, 6042 or 6112, and 6047.	100	250	6
1107: 1960 ADVANCE CATALOG, THREE-CAR DIESEL FREIGHT: 1055, 6044, 6042 or 6112, and 6047.	100	250	3
1109: 1960 ADVANCE CATALOG, THREE-CAR STEAM FREIGHT: 1060, 1060T, 6404, 3386, and 6047.	150	400	3
1111: 1948 LIONEL SCOUT SET: 1001, 1001T, 1002 blue, 1005, and 1007.	125	225	2
1112: 1948 LIONEL SCOUT SET: 1101, 1001T, 1002 blue, 1004, 1005, and 1007.			
With 1001.	100	250	1
With 1101.	125	300	2
1113: 1950 LIONEL SCOUT TRAIN: 1120, 1001T, 1002 black, 1005, and 1007.	125	225	4
1115: 1949 LIONEL SCOUT: 1110, 1001T, 1002 black, 1005, and 1007.	150	250	4
1117: 1949 LIONEL SCOUT: 1110, 1001T, 1002 black, 1005, 1004, and 1007.	150	250	4
1119: 1951-52 SCOUT THREE-CAR FREIGHT: 1110, 1001T, 1002 black, 1004, and 1007.	125	225	3
1123: 1961 ADVANCE CATALOG THREE-CAR STEAM FREIGHT: 1060, 1050T, 6406, 6042, and 6067.	125	300	5
1124: 1961 THE HAWK ADVANCE CATALOG: 1060, 1060T, 3409, 6076, and 6067 caboose.	175	500	5
1125: 1961 ADVANCE CATALOG, THREE-CAR DIESEL FREIGHT: 1065, 6630, 6480 and 6120.	200	450	5
1400: 1946 LIONEL 027 PASSENGER SET: 221, 221T, two blue 2430 Pullmans and blue 2431 Observation.	550	1,250	6
1400W: 1946 LIONEL 027 PASSENGER SET: 221, 221W, two blue 2430 Pullmans and blue 2431 Observation.	650	1,400	7
1401: 1946 LIONEL 027 FREIGHT OUTFIT: 1654, 1654T, 2452X, 2465, and 2472.	150	275	4
1401W: 1946 LIONEL 027 FREIGHT OUTFIT: 1654, 1654W, 2452X, 2465, and 2472.	250	450	6
1402: 1946 LIONEL 027 PASSENGER SET: 1666, 2466T, two green 2440s and green 2441.	500	750	6
1402W: 1946 LIONEL 027 PASSENGER SET: 1666, 2466W, two green 2440s and green 2441.	600	900	6
1403: 1946 LIONEL 027 FREIGHT TRAIN: 221, 221T, 2411, 2465, and 2472.	425	650	5
1403W: 1946 LIONEL 027 FREIGHT TRAIN: 221, 221W, 2411, 2465, and 2472.	525	775	6
1405: 1946 LIONEL 027 FREIGHT TRAIN: 1666, 2466T, 2452X, 2465, and 2472.	175	300	4

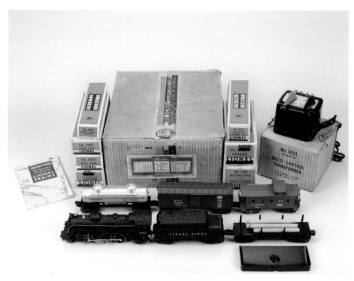

1429WS

1431

	EX	LN	RARITY
1405W: 1946 LIONEL 027 FREIGHT TRAIN: 1666, 2466W, 2452X, 2465, and 2472.	225	400	7
1407B: 1946 LIONEL 027 SWITCHER BELL OUTFIT: 1665, 2403B, 2452X, 2560, and 2419.	900	1,500	7
1409: 1946 LIONEL 027 FREIGHT TRAIN: 1666, 2466T, 3559, 2465, 3454, and 2472.	400	550	5
1409W: 1946 LIONEL 027 FREIGHT TRAIN: 1666, 2466W, 3559, 2465, 3454, and 2472.	450	650	6
1411W: 1946 FREIGHT OUTFIT: 1666, 2466WX, 2452X, 2465, 2454, and 2472.			
With Baby Ruth boxcar.	225	375	5
With Pennsylvania boxcar.	375	625	7
1413WS: 1946 LIONEL 027 FREIGHT TRAIN: 2020, 2020W, 2452X, 2465, 2454, and 2472.	350	550	4
1415WS: 1946 LIONEL 027 FREIGHT SET: 2020, 2020W, 3459, 3454, 2465, and 2472.	525	1,000	5
1417WS: 1946 LIONEL 027 FREIGHT OUTFIT: 2020, 2020W, 2465, 3451, 2560, and 2419.	750	1,100	6
1419WS: 1946 LIONEL 027 FREIGHT TRAIN: 2020, 2020W, 3459, 97, 2452X, 2560, and 2419.	900	1,300	7
1421WS: 1946 LIONEL 027 FREIGHT TRAIN: 2020, 2020W, 3451, 164, 2465, 3454, and 2472.	1,000	1,500	7
1423W: 1948-49 LIONEL THREE-CAR FREIGHT OUTFIT.			
1423W (Type I): 1948 LIONEL THREE-CAR OUTFIT: 1655, 6654W, 6452, 6465, and 6257.	150	225	3
1423W (Type II): 1949 LIONEL THREE-CAR OUTFIT: 1655, 6654W, 6462, 6465, and 6257.	150	225	3
1425B: 1948-49 SWITCHER FREIGHT.			
1425B (Type I): 1948 SWITCHER FREIGHT: 1656, 6403B, 6456 black, 6465, and 6257X.	850	1,250	3
1425B (Type II): 1949 SWITCHER FREIGHT: 1656, 6403B, 6456 black, 6465, and 6257.	850	1,250	6
1426WS: 1948-49 LIONEL PASSENGER SET: 2026, 6466WX, two green 2440 Pullmans and a green 2441 Observation.	600	1,000	5
1427WS: 1948 LIONEL THREE-CAR FREIGHT SET: 2026, 6466WX, 6465, 6454, and 6257.	250	450	3
1429WS: 1948 FOUR-CAR FREIGHT SET: 2026, 6466WX, 3451, 6465, 6454, and 6357.	200	325	3
1430WS: 1948-49 PASSENGER TRAIN: 2025, 6466WX, 2400, 2402, and 2401.	800	1,500	5
1431: 1947 LIONEL FREIGHT TRAIN: 1654, 1654T, 2452X, 2465, and 2472.	150	250	5
1431W: 1947 LIONEL FREIGHT TRAIN: 1654, 1654W, 2452X, 2465, and 2472.	175	275	5
1432: 1947 LIONEL PASSENGER SET: 221, 221T, two blue 2430 Pullmans and blue 2431 Observation.	900	1,500	5

1449WS

1457B

	EX	LN	RARITY
1432W: 1947 LIONEL PASSENGER SET: 221, 221W, two blue 2430 Pullmans and blue 2431 Observation.	900	1,500	5
1433: 1947 LIONEL FREIGHT TRAIN: 221, 221T, 2411, 2465, and 2472.	400	700	5
1433W: 1947 LIONEL FREIGHT TRAIN: 221, 221W, 2411, 2465, and 2472.	400	725	5
1434WS: 1947 PASSENGER TRAIN: 2025, 2466WX, two green 2440 Pullmans and green 2441 Observation.	400	725	5
1435WS: 1947 LIONEL FREIGHT TRAIN: 2025, 2466WX, 2452X, 2454, 2472, or 2257 caboose.	250	375	3
1437WS: 1947 LIONEL FREIGHT SET: 2025, 2466WX, 2452X, 2465, 2454, and 2472.	275	450	4
1439WS: 1947 LIONEL FREIGHT OUTFIT: 2025, 2466WX, 3559, 2465, 3454, and 2472.	425	750	5
1441WS: 1947 DE LUXE WORK OUTFIT: 2020, 2020W, 2461, 3451, 2560, and 2419.	550	900	6
1443WS: 1947 FOUR-CAR FREIGHT: 2020, 2020W, 3459, 3462, 2465, and 2472.	425	750	5
1445WS: 1948 FOUR-CAR FREIGHT: 2025, 6466WX, 3559, 6465, 6454, and 6357.	325	550	5
1447WS: 1948-49 DE LUXE WORK TRAIN.			
1447WS (Type I): 1948 2020, 6020W, 3451, 2461, 2460, and 6419.	525	950	5
1447WS (Type II): 1949 2020, 6020W, 3461, 6461, 2460, and 6419.	525	950	5
1449WS: 1948 FIVE-CAR FREIGHT OUTFIT: 2020, 6020W, 3462, 6465, 3459, 6411, and 6357.	450	800	5
1451WS: 1949 THREE-CAR FREIGHT: 2026, 6466WX, 6462, 3464, and 6257.	275	450	4
1453WS: 1949 FOUR-CAR FREIGHT: 2026, 6466WX, 3464, 6465, 3461, and 6357.	325	525	4
1455WS: 1949 FOUR-CAR 027 FREIGHT: 2025, 6466WX, 6462, 6465, 3472, and 6357.	400	750	4
1457B: 1949-50 FOUR-CAR DIESEL FREIGHT: 6220, 6462, 3464, 6520, and 6419.	625	950	5
1459WS: 1949 027 FIVE-CAR FREIGHT OUTFIT: 2020, 6020W, 6411, 3656, 6465, 3469, and 6357.	550	950	5
1461S: 1950 THREE-CAR FREIGHT WITH SMOKE: 6110, 6001T, 6002, 6004, and 6007.	150	250	2
1463W: 1950 027 THREE-CAR FREIGHT: 2036, 6466W, 6462, 6465, and 6257.	150	250	2
1463WS: 1951 027 THREE-CAR FREIGHT: 2026, 6466W, 6462, 6465, and 6257.	200	325	3
1464W (Type I): 1950 027 DIESEL THREE-CAR PULLMAN: 2023 yellow A-A, 2481, 2482 and 2483.	2,000	4,000	6
1464W (Type II): 1951 027 DIESEL THREE-CAR PULLMAN: 2023 silver A-A, 2421, 2422 and 2423 all with gray roofs.	900	1,500	4
1464W (Type III): 1952-53 THREE-CAR PULLMAN: 2033 silver A-A, 2421, 2422 and 2423 all with silver roofs.	850	1,400	3

1467W (Type I)

1505WS

1513S

	EX	LN	RARITY
1465: 1952 THREE-CAR FREIGHT: 2034, 6066T, 6032, 6035, and 6037.	150	250	2
1467W (Type I): 1950 027 DIESEL FOUR-CAR FREIGHT: 2023 yellow A-A, 6656, 6465, 6456, and 6357.	600	900	4
1467W (Type II): 1951: 2023 AA silver, 6656, 6465, 6456, and 6357.	575	875	4
1467W (Type III): 1952-53 FOUR-CAR FREIGHT: 2032 A-A, 6656, 6456, 6465, and 6357.	525	800	5
1469WS (Type I): 1950 027 FOUR-CAR FREIGHT: 2035, 6466W, 6462, 6465, 6456 black, and 6257.	225	425	3
1469WS (Type II): 1951 027 FOUR-CAR FREIGHT: 2035, 6466W, 6462, 6465, 6456 maroon, and 6257.	225	425	3
1471WS: 1950-51 FIVE-CAR FREIGHT: 2035, 6466W, 3469X, 6465, 6454, 3461X, and 6357.	350	575	3
1473WS: 1950 FOUR-CAR FREIGHT: 2046, 2046W, 3464, 6465, 6520, and 6357.	425	750	3
1475WS: 1950 FIVE-CAR FREIGHT: 2046, 2046W, 3656, 3461X, 6472, 3469X, and 6419.	575	975	6
1477S: 1951-52 027 THREE-CAR FREIGHT: 2026, 6466T, 6012, 6014 white, and 6017.	200	375	3
1479WS: 1952 027 FOUR-CAR FREIGHT: 2056, 2046W, 6462, 6465, 6456, and 6257.	425	700	3
1481WS: 1951 FIVE-CAR FREIGHT: 2035, 6466W, 3464, 6465, 3472, 6462, and 6357.	325	525	3
1483WS: 1952 FIVE-CAR FREIGHT: 2056, 2046W, 3472, 6462, 3474, 6465, and 6357.	625	950	5
1484WS: FOUR-CAR PULLMAN: 2056, 2046W, 2421, 2422, 2429, and 2423 with silver roofs.	950	1,500	6
1485WS: 027 THREE-CAR FREIGHT: 2025, 6466W, 6462, 6465, and 6257.	225	350	4
1953-54: 027 THREE-CAR FREIGHT: 1130, 6066T, 6032, 6034, and 6037.	100	150	1
1501S: 1953 027 THREE-CAR FREIGHT: 2026, 6066T, 6032, 6035, and 6037.	125	200	2
1502WS: 1953 027 THREE-CAR PULLMAN: 2055, 2046W, 2421, 2422, and 2423.	675	1,100	5
1503WS (Type I): 1953 027 FOUR-CAR FREIGHT: 2055, 6026W, 6462 black, 6456 black, 6465, and 6257.	300	500	2
1503WS (Type II): 1954 027 FOUR-CAR FREIGHT: 2055, 6026W, 6462 green, 6456 maroon, 6465, and 6257.	300	500	2
1505WS: 1953 027 FOUR-CAR FREIGHT: 2046, 2046W, 6464-1, 6462, 6415, and 6357.	400	850	4
1507WS: 1953 027 FIVE-CAR FREIGHT: 2046, 2046W, 3472, 6415, 6462, 6468, and 6357.	425	900	4
1509WS: 1953 027 FIVE-CAR FREIGHT: 2046, 2046W, 3520, 6456, 3469, 6460, and 6419.	450	800	3
1511S: 1953 027 FOUR-CAR FREIGHT: 2037, 6066T, 6032, 3474, 6035, and 6037.	300	500	4
1513S: 1954-55 027 FOUR-CAR FREIGHT: 2037, 6026T, 6012, 6014 red, 6015, and 6017.	175	300	1

1523

1536W

	EX	LN	RARITY
1515WS: 1954 027 FIVE-CAR FREIGHT: 2065, 2046W, 6415, 6462, 6464-25, 6456, and 6357.	450	750	4
1516WS: 1954 027 THREE-CAR PASSENGER: 2065, 2046W, 2434, 2432, and 2436.	950	1,725	5
1517W: 1954 027 FOUR-CAR FREIGHT: 2245P/C A-B, 6464-225, 6561, 6462 green, and 6427.	1,000	1,550	6
1519WS: 1954 027 FIVE-CAR FREIGHT: 2065, 6026W, 3461, 6462 red, 6356, 3482, and 6427.	550	975	5
1520W: 1954 027 TEXAS SPECIAL THREE-CAR PASSENGER: 2245P/C A-B, 2432, 2435 and 2436.	1,800	2,700	7
1521WS: 1954 027 FIVE-CAR FREIGHT: 2065, 2046W, 3620, 3562 black, 6561, 6460 black cA-B, and 6419.	750	1,200	5
1523: 1954 027 FOUR-CAR WORK TRAIN: 6250, 6511, 6456 gray, 6460 red cab, and 6419.	750	1,200	5
1525: 1955 027 THREE-CAR FREIGHT: 600, 6014, 6111 and 6017.	200	500	3
1527: 1955 027 THREE-CAR WORK TRAIN: 1615, 1615T, 6462, 6560 gray cab, and 6119.	400	750	5
1529: 1955 027 THREE-CAR FREIGHT: 2028, 6311, 6436 and 6257.	675	1,000	6
1531W: 1955 027 FOUR-CAR FREIGHT: 2328, 6462 red, 6456, 6465, and 6257.	575	975	6
1533WS: 1955 027 FREIGHT HAULER: 2055, 6026W, 3562 yellow, 6436, 6465, and 6357.	425	725	5
1534W: 1955 027 THREE-CAR PASSENGER: 2328, 2434, 2432 and 2436.	1,000	1,600	6
1535W: 1955 027 FOUR-CAR FREIGHT: 2243P/2243C, 6468X, 6462-25, 6436-1, and 6257-25.	800	2,200	6
1536W: 1955 027 THREE-CAR PASSENGER: 2245P/C A-B, 2432, 2432 and 2436.	1,900	3,000	6
1537WS: 1955 027 FOUR-CAR FREIGHT: 2065, 2046W, 3562 yellow, 3469, 6464-275, and 6357.	575	975	5
1538WS: 1955 027 FOUR-CAR PASSENGER: 2065, 2046W, 2435, 2434, 2432, and 2436.	900	1,500	6
1539W: 1955 027 FIVE-CAR FREIGHT: 2243 P/C A-B, 3620, 6446, 6561, 6560, and 6419.	900	1,500	5
1541WS: 1955 027 FIVE-CAR FREIGHT: 2065, 2046W, 3482, 3461, 6415, 3494, and 6427.	600	1,000	5
1542: 1956 027 THREE-CAR FREIGHT: 520, 6014 red, 6012 and 6017.	200	375	4
1543: 1956 027 THREE-CAR FREIGHT: 627, 6121, 6112 and 6017.	250	400	5
1545: 1956 027 FOUR-CAR FREIGHT: 628, 6424, 6014 red and 6257.	300	500	6
1547S: 1956 027 FREIGHT HAULER: 2018, 6026T, 6121, 6112, 6014 red, and 6257.	175	300	4
1549S: 1956 027 THREE-CAR WORK TRAIN: 1615, 1615T, 6262, 6560, and 6119 orange.	800	1,350	5
1551S: 1956 027 FOUR-CAR FREIGHT: 621, 6362, 6425, 6562, and 6257.	400	700	5

1561WS

1590

	EX	LN	RARITY
1552: 1956 027 PASSENGER: 629, 2434, 2432 and 2436.	1,100	1,900	7
1553W: 1956 027 FIVE-CAR FREIGHT: 2338, 6430, 6462 red, 6464-425, 6346, and 6257.	700	1,100	5
1555WS: 027 FREIGHT HAULER: 2018, 6026W, 3361, 6464-400, 6462 red, and 6257.	350	600	4
1557W: 1956 027 FIVE-CAR WORK TRAIN: 621, 6436, 6511, 3620, 6560, and 6119.	500	950	5
1559W: 1956 027 FIVE-CAR FREIGHT: 2338, 6414, and 3562 yellow, 6362, 3494-275, and 6357.	750	1,200	5
1561WS: 1956 027 FIVE-CAR FREIGHT: 2065, 6026W, 6430, 3424, 6262, 6562, and 6257.	575	975	5
1562W: 1956 027 FOUR-CAR PASSENGER: 2328, 2442, 2442, 2444, and 2446.	1,800	3,000	6
1563W: 1956 027 FIVE-CAR FREIGHT: 2240 P/C A-B, 6467, 3562 yellow, 3620, 6414, and 6357.	1,700	2,950	6
1565W: 1956 027 FIVE-CAR FREIGHT: 2065, 6026W, 3662, 3650, 6414, 6346, and 6357.	550	975	6
1567W: 027 FIVE-CAR FREIGHT: 2243 P/C A-B, 3356, 3424, 6672, 6430, and 6357.	975	1,600	6
1569: 1957 027 FOUR-CAR FREIGHT: 202, 6014 white, 6111, 6112, and 6017.	300	500	4
1571: 1957 027 FIVE-CAR FREIGHT: 625, 6424, 6476, 6121, 6112, and 6017.	425	700	5
1573: 1957 027 FIVE-CAR FREIGHT: 250, 250T, 6025, 6112, 6464-425, 6476, and 6017.	250	400	5
1575: 1957 027 FIVE-CAR FREIGHT: 205 P/T A-A, 6111, 6121, 6112, 6560, and 6119.	350	600	5
1577S: 1957 027 SIX-CAR FREIGHT: 2018, 1130T, 6121, 6464-475, 6111, 6014 red, 6112, and 6017.	250	400	5
1578S: 1957 027 THREE-CAR PASSENGER: 2018,1130T, 2434, 2432, and 2436.	525	925	7
1579S: 1957 027 SEVEN-CAR FREIGHT: 2037, 1130T, 6111, 6025, 6476, 6468, 6112, 6121, and 6017.	300	500	5
1581: 1957 027 SEVEN-CAR FREIGHT: 611, 6476, 6024, 6424, 6464-650, 6025, 6560, and 6119.	550	975	5
1583WS: 1957 027 SIX-CAR FREIGHT: 2037, 6026W, 6482, 6112, 6646, 6121, 6476 black, and 6017.	250	400	4
1585W: 1957 027 NINE-CAR FREIGHT TRAIN: 602, 6014 white, 6121, 6025, 6464-525, 6112, 6024, 6476 gray, 6111, and 6017.	425	700	5
1586: 1957 027 THREE-CAR PASSENGER: 204P/T A-A, 2432, 2432 and 2436.	700	1,200	6
1587S: 1957-58 LADY LIONEL PASTEL TRAIN SET: 2037-500, 1130T-500, 6462-500, 6464-515, 6436-500, 6464-510, and 6427-500.	3,000	5,000	6
1589WS: 1957 027 SEVEN-CAR FREIGHT: 2037, 6026W, 6464-450, 6111, 6025 orange, 6024, 6424, 6112, and 6017.	500	750	5
1590: 1958 027 FOUR-CAR STEAM FREIGHT: 249, 250T, 6014 red Bosco, 6151, 6112, and 6017.	300	500	4

1599

1605W

1607WS

1611

	EX	LN	RARITY
1591: 1958 U.S. MARINE LAND & SEA LIMITED: 212, 6809, 6807, 6803, and 6017-50.	1,000	1,850	6
1593: 1958 FIVE-CAR UP DIESEL WORK TRAIN: 613, 6476, 6818, 6660, 6112, and 6119.	550	1,100	5
1595: 1958 027 MARINE BATTLEFRONT SPECIAL: 1625, 1625T, 6804, 6808, 6806, and 6017 gray.	1,600	2,800	7
1597S: 1958 027 SIX-CAR COAL KING SMOKING FREIGHTER: 2018, 1130T, 6014 orange, 6818, 6476 red, 6025 black, 6112 blue, and 6017.	325	600	5
1599: 1958 027 SIX-CAR TEXAS SPECIAL FREIGHT: 210 A-A, 6801-50 with yellow hull boat, 6112-1 black, 6014 orange Bosco or red Frisco, 6424-60, 6465-60 gray, and 6017.	400	825	4
1600: 1958 027 THREE-CAR BURLINGTON PASSENGER: 216, 6572, 2432 and 2436.	950	1,700	7
1601W: 1958 027 FIVE-CAR DIESEL FREIGHT: 2337, 6800, 6464-425, 6801, 6810, and 6017.	900	1,600	5
1603WS: 1958 027 FIVE-CAR WHISTLING MOUNTAIN CLIMBER STEAM FREIGHT: 2037, 6026W, 6424, 6014-60 white Bosco, 6818, 6112, and 6017.	400	750	5
1605W: 1958 027 SIX-CAR SANTA FE DIESEL FREIGHT: 208 AA, 6800, 6464-425, 6801, 6477, 6802, and 6017.	900	1,600	5
1607WS: 1958 027 SIX-CAR TROUBLE SHOOTER WORK SET: 2037, 6026W, 6465, 6818, 6464-425, 6112, 6660, and 6119.	475	800	5
1608W: 1958 027 FOUR-CAR MERCHANTS LIMITED DIESEL PASSENGER: 209P/T A-A, 2434, 2432, 2432, and 2436.	1,500	2,700	7
1609: 1959-60 027 THREE-CAR STEAM FREIGHT: 246, 1130T, 6162-25 blue, 6476 red, and 6057.			
Tan conventional box.	200	450	4
Display box with dividers.	125	200	2
Display box with die-cut filler.	150	225	2
Display box with individual component boxes.	150	250	3
1611: 1959 027 FOUR-CAR ALASKAN FREIGHT: 614, 6825, 6162-50, 6465 black, and 6027.			
Display box.	575	950	4
Tan conventional box.	650	1,400	6
1612: 1959-60 THE GENERAL OLD-TIMER OUTFIT: 1862, 1862T, 1866 and 1865.			
Display box.	350	600	1
Tan conventional box.	450	900	4
1613S: 1959 FOUR-CAR B & O STEAM FREIGHT: 247, 247T, 6826, 6819, 6821, and 6017.	300	500	5

1615

1633

1635WS

1639WS

	EX	LN	RARITY
1615: 1959 FIVE-CAR BOSTON & MAINE DIESEL FREIGHT: 217P/C A-B, 6800, 6464-475, 6812, 6825, and 6017-100.			
Display box.	575	975	5
Tan box.	675	1,150	6
1617S: 1959 FIVE-CAR BUSY BEAVER STEAM WORK TRAIN: 2018, 1130T, 6816, 6536, 6812, 6670, and 6119.	850	1,500	5
1619W: 1959 FIVE-CAR SANTA FE DIESEL FREIGHT: 218P/T A-A, 6819, 6802, 6801, 6519, and 6017-185 gray.	450	900	4
1621WS: 1959 FIVE-CAR CONSTRUCTION SPECIAL STEAM FREIGHT: 2037, 6026W, 6825, 6519, 6062, 6464-475, and 6017.	300	525	4
1623W: 1959 FIVE-CAR NP DIESEL FREIGHT: 2349, 3512, 3435, 6424, 6062, and 6017.	1,200	2,100	7
1625WS: 1959 FIVE-CAR ACTION KING STEAM FREIGHT: 2037, 6026W, 6636, 3512, 6470, 6650, and 6017.	400	700	5
1626W: 1959 FOUR-CAR SANTA FE DIESEL PASSENGER: 208P/T A-A, 3428, 2412 blue stripe, 2412 blue stripe, and 2416 blue stripe.	750	1,250	5
1627S: 1960 027 THREE-CAR STEAM FREIGHT: 244, 244T, 6062, 6825, and 6017.	90	150	1
1629: 1960 FOUR-CAR C & O DIESEL FREIGHT: 225, 6650, 6470, 6819, and 6219.	300	500	1
1631WS: 1960 FOUR-CAR INDUSTRIAL STEAM FREIGHT: 243, 243W, 6519, 6812, 6465, and 6017.	300	500	2
1633: 1960 LAND-SEA-AIR TWO-UNIT DIESEL FREIGHT: 224P/C A-B, 6544, 6830, 6820, and 6017-200.	900	1,600	4
1635WS: 1960 FIVE-CAR HEAVY-DUTY SPECIAL STEAM FREIGHT: 2037, 243W, 6361, 6826, 6636, 6821, and 6017.	450	850	5
1637W: 1960 FIVE-CAR TWIN UNIT DIESEL FREIGHT: 218 P/T A-A, 6475, 6175, 6464-475, 6801, and 6017-185.	500	950	5
1639WS: 1960 SIX-CAR POWER HOUSE SPECIAL STEAM FREIGHT: 2037, 243W, 6816, 6817, 6812, 6530, 6560, and 6119.	1,750	2,800	7
1640W: 1960 FIVE-CAR PRESIDENTIAL CAMPAIGN SPECIAL: 218 P/T A-A, 3428, two 2412s blue stripe, 2416 blue stripe, and 1640-100.	650	1,000	4
1641: 1961 THREE-CAR HEADLINER STEAM FREIGHT: 246, 244T, 3362, 6162, and 6057.	90	150	3
1642: 1961 THREE-CAR CIRCUS SPECIAL STEAM FREIGHT: 244, 1130T, 3376, 6405, and 6119.	175	300	3
1643: 1961 FOUR-CAR SKY-SCOUT DIESEL FREIGHT: 230, 3509, 6050, 6175, and 6058.	275	475	3
1644: 1961 FRONTIER SPECIAL GENERAL PASSENGER: 1862, 1862T, 3370, 1866, and 1865.	475	700	3
1645: 1961 027 FOUR-CAR DIESEL FREIGHT: 229, 3410, 6465, 6825, and 6059.	240	400	4

1651

2115WS

	EX	LN	RARITY
1646: 1961 FOUR-CAR UTILITY STEAM FREIGHT: 233, 233W, 6162, 6343, 6476 red, and 6017.	350	600	2
1647: 1961 FREEDOM FIGHTER MISSILE LAUNCHER OUTFIT: 45, 3665, 3519, 6830, 6448, and 6814.	900	1,475	6
1648: 1961 FIVE-CAR SUPPLY LINE STEAM FREIGHT: 2037, 233W, 6062, 6465, 6519, 6476 red, and 6017.	250	400	3
1649: 1961 027 FIVE-CAR TWO-UNIT DIESEL FREIGHT: 218P/C A-B, 6343, 6445, 6475, 6405, and 6017.	525	900	6
1650: 1961 FIVE-CAR GUARDIAN STEAM FREIGHT: 2037, 233W, 6544, 6470, 3330, 3419, and 6017.	450	800	6
1651: 1961 FOUR-CAR ALL PASSENGER DIESEL: 218 P/T A-A, two 2412s blue stripe and 2416 blue stripe.	750	1,200	4
1800: 1959-60 THE GENERAL FRONTIER PACK: 1862, 1862T, 1877, 1866, 1865, and General Story Book.	400	725	3
1805: 1960 LAND-SEA-AND AIR GIFT PACK: 45, 3429, 3820, 6640, and 6824.	1,750	3,000	5
1809: 1961 THE WESTERN GIFT PACK: 244, 1130T, 3370, 3376,1877, and 6017.	300	500	3
1810: 1961 THE SPACE AGE GIFT PACK: 231, 3665, 3519, 3820, and 6017.	550	975	3
2100: 1946 O-GAUGE THREE-CAR PASSENGER: 224, 2466T, two brown 2442s and brown 2443.	550	950	7
2100W: 1946 O-GAUGE THREE-CAR PASSENGER: 224, 2466W, two brown 2442s and a brown 2443.	500	800	5
2101: 1946 O-GAUGE THREE-CAR FREIGHT: 224, 2466T, 2555, 2452, and 2457.	400	675	6
2101W: 1946 O-GAUGE THREE-CAR FREIGHT: 224, 2466W, 2555, 2452, and 2457.	300	500	5
2103W: 1946 O-GAUGE FOUR-CAR FREIGHT: 224, 2466W, 2458, 3559, 2555, and 2457.	425	1,000	5
2105WS: 1946 THREE-CAR FREIGHT OUTFIT: 671, 671W, 2555, 2454, and 2457.	400	1,000	5
2110WS: 1946 THREE-CAR PASSENGER: 671, 671W and three 2625s.	1,750	2,975	7
2111WS: 1946 FOUR-CAR FREIGHT: 671, 671W, 3459, 2411, 2460, and 2420.	825	1,400	7
2113WS: 1946 O-GAUGE THREE-CAR FREIGHT OUTFIT: 726, 2426W, 2855, 3854, and 2457.	2,000	3,200	7
2114WS: 1946 O-GAUGE THREE-CAR PASSENGER OUTFIT: 726, 2426W and three 2625 "Irvington" Pullmans.	2,500	4,000	6
2115WS: 1946 O-GAUGE FOUR-CAR WORK TRAIN WITH SMOKE: 726, 2426W, 2458, 3451, 2460, and 2420.	1,350	2,400	7
2120S: 1947 THREE-CAR DELUXE PASSENGER: 675, 2466T, two brown 2442s and a brown 2443.	500	875	6
2120WS: 1947 THREE-CAR DELUXE PASSENGER: 675, 2466WX, two brown 2442s and a brown 2443.	525	900	4
2121S: 1947 THREE-CAR FREIGHT: 675, 2466T, 2452, 2555, and 2457.	375	550	6

2140WS

2141WS (Type II)

	EX	LN	RARITY
2121WS: 1947 THREE-CAR FREIGHT: 675, 2466WX, 2452, 2555, and 2457.	400	575	5
2123WS: 1947 FOUR-CAR FREIGHT: 675, 2466WX, 2458, 3559, 2555, and 2457.	450	800	5
2124W: 1947 THREE-CAR PASSENGER: 2332, 2625 Irvington, 2625 Madison and 2625 Manhattan.			
With green GG-1.	3,000	5,000	5
With black GG-1.	4,000	7,300	7
2125WS: 1947 FOUR-CAR FREIGHT: 671, 671W, 2411, 2454, 2452, and 2457.	575	975	5
2126WS: 1947 THREE-CAR PASSENGER: 671, 671W, 2625 Irvington, 2625 Madison, and 2625 Manhattan.	1,700	3,000	5
2127WS: 1947 LIONEL WORK TRAIN: 671, 671W, 3459, 2461, 2460, and 2420.	750	1,250	5
2129WS: 1947 FOUR-CAR FREIGHT: 726, 2426W, 3854, 2411, 2855, and 2457.	2,100	3,500	6
2131WS: 1947 FOUR-CAR DE LUXE WORK TRAIN: 726, 2426W, 3462, 3451, 2460, and 2420.	1,100	1,900	5
2133W: 1948 TWIN DIESEL O-GAUGE FREIGHT: 2333 P/T A-A, 2458, 3459, 2555, and 2357.			
New York Central rubber stamped.	1,000	2,500	6
New York Central heat stamped.	700	2,000	5
Santa Fe.	800	2,200	5
2135WS (Type I): 1948 THREE-CAR FREIGHT: 675, 2466WX, 2456, 2411, and 2357.	325	525	4
2135WS (Type II): 1949 THREE-CAR FREIGHT: 675, 6466WX, 6456, 6411, and 6457.	325	525	4
2136WS (Type I): 1948 THREE-CAR PASSENGER: 675, 2466WX, two brown 2442s and a brown 2443.	550	900	5
2136WS (Type II): 1949 THREE-CAR PASSENGER: 675, 6466WX, two brown 6442s and a brown 6443.	500	850	4
2137WS: 1948 FOUR-CAR DELUXE FREIGHT: 675, 2466WX, 2458, 3459, 2456, and 2357.	400	700	4
2139W (Type I): 1948 FOUR-CAR FREIGHT: 2332, 3451, 2458, 2456, and 2357.	1,500	2,500	4
2139W (Type II): 1948 O-GAUGE FOUR-CAR FREIGHT OUTFIT: 2332, 6456, 3464, 3461, and 6457.	1,400	2,400	4
2140WS: 1948-49 THREE-CAR DE LUXE PASSENGER: 671, 2671W, 2400, 2402, and 2401.	900	1,500	5
2141WS (Type I): 1948 FOUR-CAR FREIGHT: 671, 2671W, 3451, 3462, 2456, and 2357.	500	775	4
2141WS (Type II): 1949 FOUR-CAR FREIGHT: 671, 2671W, 3461, 3472, 6456, and 6457.	500	775	4
2143WS: 1948 FOUR-CAR DELUXE WORK TRAIN: 671, 2671W, 3459, 2461, 2460, and 2420.	700	1,200	5

2150WS

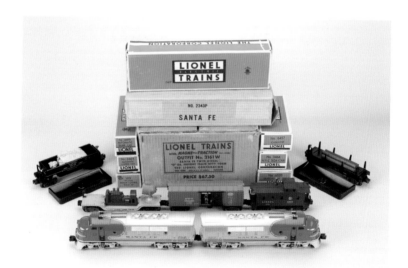

2161W

	EX	LN	RARITY
2144W: 1948-49 THREE-CAR DELUXE PASSENGER OUTFIT: 2332, 2625, 2627 and 2628.	2,400	4,000	5
2145WS: 1948 FOUR-CAR FREIGHT: 726, 2426W, 3462, 2411, 2460, and 2357.	850	1,400	5
2146WS: 1948-49 THREE-CAR PULLMAN: 726, 2426W, 2625, 2627, and 2628.	2,400	4,000	7
2147WS: 1949 FOUR-CAR FREIGHT SET: 675, 6466WX, 3472, 6465, 3469, and 6457.	350	600	3
2148WS: 1950 O-GAUGE THREE-CAR DELUXE PULLMAN: 773, 2426W, 2625, 2627, and 2628.	4,700	8,500	6
2149B: 1949 O-GAUGE FOUR-CAR DIESEL WORK TRAIN: 622, 6520, 3469, 2460, and 6419.	700	1,100	5
2150WS: 1950 O-GAUGE DELUXE PASSENGER: 681, 2671W, 2421, 2422, and 2423.	800	1,300	5
2151W: 1949 O-GAUGE FIVE-CAR DIESEL: 2333 P/T A-A, 3464, 6555, 3469, 6520, and 6457.			
New York Central.	1,100	1,900	4
Santa Fe.	1,200	2,000	4
2153WS: 1949 FOUR-CAR DELUXE WORK TRAIN: 671, 2671W, 3469, 6520, 2460, and 6419.	600	1,000	4
2155WS: 1949 FOUR-CAR FREIGHT: 726, 2426W, 6411, 3656, 2460, and 6457.	800	1,300	5
2159W: 1950 FIVE-CAR FREIGHT: 2330, 3464, 6462, 3461X, 6456, and 6457.	2,000	3,500	6
2161W: 1950 SF TWIN DIESEL FREIGHT: 2343 A-A, 3469X, 3464, 3461X, 6520, and 6457.	1,500	2,500	4
2163WS (Type I): 1950 FOUR-CAR FREIGHT: 736, 2671WX, 6472, 6462, 6555, and 6457.	600	925	4
2163WS (Type II): 1951 FOUR-CAR FREIGHT: 736, 2671WX, 6472, 6462, 6465, and 6457.	575	900	4
2165WS: 1950 O-GAUGE FOUR-CAR FREIGHT: 736, 2671WX, 3472, 6456, 3461X, and 6457.	600	1,000	4
2167WS: 1950-51 THREE-CAR FREIGHT: 681, 2671W, 6462, 3464, and 6457.	400	650	4
2169WS: 1950 FIVE-CAR FREIGHT WITH SMOKE AND WHISTLE: 773, 2426W, 3656, 6456, 3469X, 6411, and 6457.	2,700	4,500	6
2171W: 1950 NYC TWIN DIESEL FREIGHT: 2344 A-A, 3469X, 3464, 3461X, 6520, and 6457.	1,200	2,000	4
2173WS (Type I): 1950 FOUR-CAR FREIGHT: 681, 2671W, 3472, 6555, 3469X, and 6457.	500	775	4
2173WS (Type II): 1951 FOUR-CAR FREIGHT: 681, 2671W, 3472, 6465, 3469X, and 6457.	500	775	4
2175W (Type I): 1950 FIVE-CAR SANTA FE TWIN DIESEL FREIGHT: 2343 A-A, 6456 black, 3464, 6555, 6462, and 6457.	1,200	2,000	3
2175W (Type II): 1951 FIVE-CAR SANTA FE TWIN DIESEL FREIGHT: 2343 A-A, 6456 maroon, 3464, 6465, 6462, and 6457.	1,200	2,000	3

2177WS

2193W

2219W

2221WS

	EX	LN	RARITY
2177WS: 1952 THREE-CAR FREIGHT: 675, 2046W, 6462, 6465, and 6457.	300	500	5
2179WS: 1952 FOUR-CAR FREIGHT: 671rr, 2046WX, 3464, 6465, 6462, and 6457.	400	700	4
2183WS: 1952 FOUR-CAR FREIGHT: 726rr, 2046W, 3464, 6462, 6465, and 6457.	550	900	4
2185W (Type I): 1950 FIVE-CAR NYC TWIN DIESEL FREIGHT: 2344 A-A, 6456 black, 3464, 6555, 6462, and 6457.	1,200	2,000	3
2185W (Type II): 1951 FIVE-CAR NYC TWIN DIESEL FREIGHT: 2344 A-A, 6456 maroon, 3464, 6465, 6462, and 6457.	1,200	2,000	3
2187WS: 1952 FIVE-CAR FREIGHT: 671rr, 2046WX, 6462, 3472, 6456 maroon, 3469, and 6457.	500	850	5
2189WS: 1952 FIVE-CAR TRANSCONTINENTAL FAST FREIGHT: 726rr, 2046W, 3520, 3656, 6462, 3461, and 6457.	600	1,000	5
2190W (Type I): 1952 FOUR-CAR SUPER SPEEDLINER PASSENGER: 2343 A-A, 2533, 2532, 2534, and 2531.	1,800	3,000	3
2190W (Type II): 1953 FOUR-CAR SUPER SPEEDLINER PASSENGER: 2353 A-A, 2533, 2532, 2534, and 2531.	1,800	3,000	3
2191W: 1952 FOUR-CAR DIESEL FREIGHT: 2343 A-A, 2343C B-Unit, 6462, 6656, 6456, and 6457.	1,500	2,500	4
2193W: 1952 FOUR-CAR DIESEL FREIGHT: 2344 A-A, 2344C B-Unit, 6462, 6656, 6456, and 6457.	1,600	2,650	4
2201WS (Type I): 1953 FOUR-CAR FREIGHT: 685, 6026W, 6462, 6464-50, 6465, and 6357.	750	1,200	5
2201WS (Type II): 1954 FIREBALL EXPRESS: 665, 6026W, 6462, 6464-50, 6465, and 6357.	650	1,100	4
2203WS: 1953 FOUR-CAR FREIGHT: 681, 2046WX, 3520, 6415, 6464-25, and 6417.	725	1,200	4
2205WS: 1953 FIVE-CAR FREIGHT: 736, 2046W, 3484, 6415, 6468 blue, 6456, and 6417.	700	1,150	4
2207W: 1953 TRIPLE DIESEL FREIGHT: 2353 A-A, 2343C B-Unit, 3484, 6415, 6462, and 6417.	1,500	2,500	4
2209W: 1953 TRIPLE DIESEL FREIGHT: 2354 AA, 2344C B-Unit, 3484, 6415, 6462, and 6417.	1,550	2,600	4
2211WS: 1953 FOUR-CAR FREIGHT: 681, 2046WX, 3656, 3461, 6464-75, and 6417.	700	1,200	5
2213WS: 1953 FIVE-CAR FREIGHT: 736, 2046W, 3461, 3520, 3469, 6460, and 6419.	575	975	4
2217WS: 1954 O-GAUGE FREIGHT MASTER: 682, 2046WX, 3562 gray, 6464-175, 6356, and 6417.	1,000	1,600	5
2219W: 1954 O-GAUGE THE THUNDERBIRD: 2321, 6415, and 6462 green, 6464-50, 6456 gray, and 6417.	1,200	2,000	5
2221WS: 1954 O-GAUGE DIAMOND EXPRESS: 646, 2046W, 3620, 3469, 6468 blue, 6456 gray, and 6417.	600	1,000	4
2222WS: 1954 O-GAUGE THE MAINLINER: 646, 2046W, 2530, 2532, and 2531.	1,600	2,700	5
2223W: 1954 O-GAUGE THE BIG HAUL: 2321, 3482, 3461, 6464-100, 6462 red, and 6417.	2,400	4,000	6

2225WS

2234W

2234W

2251W

	EX	LN	RARITY
2225WS: 1954 O-GAUGE THE TROUBLESHOOTER: 736, 2046W, 3461, 3620, 3562 gray, 6460 black cab, and 6419.	750	1,200	5
2227W: 1954 O-GAUGE GOLDEN WEST SPECIAL: 2353 A-A, 3562 gray, 6356, 6456 red, 6468 blue, and 6417.	1,500	2,500	4
2229W: 1954 O-GAUGE WATER LEVEL LIMITED: 2354 A-A, 3562 gray, 6356, 6456 red, 6468 blue, and 6417.	1,500	2,500	5
2231W: 1954 O-GAUGE GREAT SOUTHERN FREIGHT: 2356 A-A, 2356C B-Unit, 6561, 6511, 3482, 6415, and 6417.	2,400	4,000	5
2234W: 1954 FOUR-CAR SUPER-STREAMLINER: 2353 A-A, 2530, 2532, 2533, and 2531.	2,200	3,800	4
2235W: 1955 O-GAUGE FOUR-CAR FREIGHT: 2338, 6436, and 6362, 6560 red, and 6419.	550	900	3
2237WS: 1955 O-GAUGE THREE-CAR FREIGHT: 665, 6026W, 3562 yellow, 6415, and 6417.	400	750	3
2239W: 1955 O-GAUGE STREAK-LINER: 2363 P/C A-B, 6672, 6464-125, 6414, and 6517.	1,800	3,000	5
2241WS: 1955 O-GAUGE FREIGHT SNORTER: 646, 2046W, 3359, 6446, 3620, and 6417.	600	1,000	5
2243W: 1955 O-GAUGE FIVE-CAR FREIGHT: 2321, 3662, 6511, 6462 red, 6464-300, and 6417.	1,500	2,500	5
2244W: 1955 THREE-CAR PASSENGER: 2367 P/C A-B, 2530, 2533 and 2531.	4,000	6,500	6
2245WS: 1955 O-GAUGE FIVE-CAR FREIGHT: 682, 2046W, 3562, 6436, 6561, 6560, and 6419.	800	1,250	5
2247W: 1955 O-GAUGE FIVE-CAR FREIGHT: 2367 P/C A-B, 6462 red, 3662, 6464-150, 3361, and 6517.	2,500	4,000	5
2249WS: 1955 O-GAUGE FIVE-CAR FREIGHT: 736, 2046W, 3359, 3562 yellow, 6414, 6464-275, and 6517.	900	1,500	5
2251W: 1955 O-GAUGE FIVE-CAR FREIGHT: 2331, 3359, 3562 yellow, 6414, 6464-275, and 6517.	2,500	4,000	5
2253W: 1955 O-GAUGE FIVE-CAR FREIGHT: 2340-25 green, 3620, 6414, 3361, 6464-300, and 6417.	2,700	4,500	5
2254W: 1955 THE CONGRESSIONAL: 2340-1 Tuscan, 2544, 2543, 2542, and 2541.	5,500	9,500	5
2255W: 1956 O-GAUGE FOUR-CAR WORK TRAIN: 601, 3424, 6362, 6560, and 6119 orange.	600	1,000	4
2257WS: 1956 O-GAUGE FIVE-CAR FREIGHT: 665, 2046W, 3361, 6346, 6467, 6462 red, and 6427.	500	750	3
2259W: 1956 O-GAUGE FIVE-CAR FREIGHT: 2350, 6464-425, 6430, 3650, 6511, and 6427.	850	1,400	3
2261WS: 1956 O-GAUGE FREIGHT HAULER: 646, 2046W, 3562 yellow, 6414, 6436, 6376, and 6417.	575	950	5
2263W: 1956 O-GAUGE FIVE-CAR FREIGHT: 2350, 3359, 6468, 6414, 3662, and 6517.	900	1,500	5
2265WS: 1956 O-GAUGE FIVE-CAR FREIGHT: 736, 2046W, 3620, 6430, 3424, 6467, and 6517.	750	1,200	5
2267W: 1956 FIVE-CAR FREIGHT: 2331, 3562 yellow, 3359, 3361, 6560, and 6419.	1,600	2,650	5

2289WS

2292WS

2505W

2507W

	EX	LN	RARITY
2269W: 1956 O-GAUGE FIVE-CAR FREIGHT: 2368 P/C A-B, 3356, 6518, 6315, 3361, and 6517.	4,000	6,750	7
2270W: 1956 THREE-CAR JERSEY CENTRAL PASSENGER: 2341, 2533, 2532 and 2531.	5,600	9,000	7
2271W: 1956 O-GAUGE FIVE-CAR FREIGHT: 2360-25 green, 3424, 3662, 6414, 6418, and 6417.	3,000	5,000	5
2273W: 1956 SIX-CAR MILWAUKEE ROAD DIESEL FREIGHT: 2378P/C A-B, 342, 6342, 3562 yellow, 3662, 3359, and 6517.	4,000	6,500	6
2274W: 1956 THE GREAT CONGRESSIONAL: 2360-1 Tuscan, 2544, 2543, 2542, and 2541.	5,000	8,500	7
2275W: 1957 O-GAUGE FOUR-CAR FREIGHT: 2339, 3444, 6464-475, 6425, and 6427.	750	1,200	3
2276W: 1957 BUDD RDC COMMUTER SET: 404 and 2559.	3,000	5,000	5
2277WS: 1957 O-GAUGE FOUR-CAR WORK TRAIN: 665, 2046W, 3650, 6446, 6560, and 6119.	550	900	5
2279W: 1957 O-GAUGE FIVE-CAR FREIGHT: 2350, 6464-425, 6424, 3424, 6477, and 6427.	825	1,300	4
2281W: 1957 O-GAUGE FIVE-CAR FREIGHT: 2243 A-B, 3562 orange, 6464-150, 3361, 6560, and 6119.	1,200	2,000	3
2283WS: 1957 O-GAUGE FIVE-CAR FREIGHT: 646, 2046W, 3424, 3361, 6464-525, 6562 black, and 6357.	600	1,000	5
2285W: 1957 O-GAUGE FIVE-CAR FREIGHT: 2331, 6418, 6414, 3662, 6425, and 6517.	1,800	3,000	6
2287W: 1957 O-GAUGE FIVE-CAR FREIGHT: 2351, 342, 6342, 6464-500, 3650, 6315, and 6427.	1,800	3,000	6
2289WS: 1957 SUPER 0 FIVE-CAR FREIGHT: 736, 2046W, 3359, 3494-275, 3361, 6430, and 6427.	750	1,250	5
2291W: 1957 SUPER 0 FIVE-CAR FREIGHT: 2379 P/C A-B, 3562 orange, 3530, 3444, 6464-525, and 6657.	3,000	5,000	6
2292WS: 1957 SUPER 0 STEAM LUXURY LINER: 646, 2046W, 2530, 2533, 2532, and 2531.	1,500	2,500	4
2293W: 1957 FIVE-CAR FREIGHT: 2360 Tuscan, 3662, 3650, 6414, 6518, and 6417.	2,900	4,900	6
2295WS: 1957 SIX-CAR STEAM FREIGHT: 746, 746W, 342, 6342, 3530, 3361, 6560, and 6419-100.	3,000	5,000	7
2296W: 1957 SUPER 0 DIESEL LUXURY LINER: 2373 P/T A-A, 2552, 2552, 2552, and 2551.	6,000	10,000	6
2297WS: 1957 THE 16 WHEELER CLASS J: 746, 746W, 264, 6264, 3356, 345, 6342, 3662, and 6517.	3,300	5,500	7
2501W: 1958 SUPER 0 WORK TRAIN: 2348, 6464-525, 6802, 6560, and 6119.	750	1,400	5
2502W: 1958 SUPER 0 RAIL-DIESEL COMMUTER: 400, 2559 and 2550.	2,000	4,000	8
2503WS: 1958 TIMBERLAND SPECIAL FREIGHT: 665, 2046W, 3361, 6434, 6801, 6536, and 6357.	550	1,000	5
2505W: 1958 SUPER 0 FIVE-CAR FREIGHT: 2329, 6805, 6519, 6800, 6464-500, and 6357.	1,500	2,750	5
2507W: 1958 SUPER 0 FIVE-CAR DIESEL FREIGHT: 2242P/C A-B, 3444, 6464-425, 6424, 6468-25, and 6357.	2,000	3,200	6

2527

2528WS

2535WS

	EX	LN	RARITY
2509WS: 1958 THE OWL FIVE-CAR FREIGHT: 665, 2046W, 6414, 3650, 6464-475, 6805, and 6357.	800	1,300	5
2511W: 1958 SUPER 0 FIVE-CAR ELECTRIC WORK TRAIN: 2352, 3562 orange, 3424, 3361, 6560, and 6119.	1,200	2,100	6
2513W: 1958 SUPER 0 SIX-CAR FREIGHT TRAIN: 2329, 6556, 6425, 6414, 6434, 3359, and 6427-60.	2,000	3,700	7
2515WS: 1958 FIVE-CAR MAINLINER STEAM FREIGHT: 646, 2046W, 3662, 6424, 3444, 6800, and 6427.	800	1,500	5
2517W: 1958 SUPER 0 FIVE-CAR DIESEL FREIGHT: 2379 A-B, 6519, 6805, 6434, 6800, and 6657.	2,400	4,100	7
2518W: 1958 SUPER 0 THREE-CAR PASSENGER: 2352, 2533, 2534 and 2531.	1,500	2,600	7
2519W: 1958 SUPER 0 SIX-CAR DIESEL FREIGHT: 2331, 6434, 3530, 6801, 6414, 6464-275, and 6557.	2,000	3,200	5
2521WS: 1958 SUPER 0 SIX-CAR FREIGHT: 746, 746W, 6805, 3361, 6430, 3356, and 6557.	2,500	4,200	6
2523W: 1958 SUPER 0 SUPER CHIEF FREIGHT: 2383 A-A, 264, 6264, 6434, 6800, 3662, and 6517.	1,800	3,000	6
2525WS: 1958 SUPER 0 SIX-CAR WORK TRAIN: 746, 746W, 345, 342, 6519, 6518, 6560, and 6419-100.	3,000	5,000	4
2526W: 1958 SUPER CHIEF PASSENGER: 2383 P/T A-A, 2530, 2532, 2532, and 2531.	1,800	3,000	4
2527: 1959-60 SUPER 0 MISSILE LAUNCHER OUTFIT: 44, 3419, 6844, 6823, 6814, and 943.			
Yellow display box.	700	1,200	4
Orange and white display box.	750	1,300	4
Tan conventional box.	825	1,350	5
2528WS: 1959-61 FIVE-STAR FRONTIER SPECIAL OUTFIT: 1872, 1872T, 1877, 1876, and 1875W.			
Tan conventional box.	900	1,600	4
Display box with die-cut filler.	750	1,350	3
Display box with individual component boxes.	825	1,475	3
2529W: 1959 FIVE-CAR VIRGINIAN RECTIFIER WORK TRAIN: 2329, 3512, 6819, 6812, 6560, and 6119.	1,250	2,100	5
2531WS: 1959 SUPER 0 FIVE-CAR STEAM FREIGHT: 637, 2046W, 3435, 6817, 6636, 6825, and 6119.	1,250	2,100	6
2533W: 1959 FIVE-CAR GREAT NORTHERN ELECTRIC FREIGHT: 2358, 6650, 6414, 3444, 6470, and 6357.	1,800	3,100	7
2535WS: 1959 SUPER 0 FIVE-CAR HUDSON STEAM FREIGHT: 665, 2046W, 3434, 6823, 3672, 6812, and 6357.	1,000	1,700	5
2537W: 1959 FIVE-CAR NEW HAVEN DIESEL FREIGHT: 2242 P/C A-B, 3435, 3650, 6464-275, 6819, and 6427.	2,500	4,200	7

2547WS

2549W

4109WS

	EX	LN	RARITY
2539WS: 1959 FIVE-CAR HUDSON STEAM FREIGHT: 665, 2046W, 3361, 464, 6464-825, 3512, 6812, and 6357.	1,500	2,600	6
2541W: 1959 FIVE-CAR SUPER CHIEF FREIGHT: 2383 P/T A-A, 3356, 3512, 6519, 6816, and 6427.	2,300	3,900	6
2543WS: 1959 SIX-CAR BERKSHIRE STEAM FREIGHT: 736, 2046W, 264, 6264, 3435, 6823, 6434, 6812, and 6557.	2,000	3,500	7
2544W: 1959-60 FOUR-CAR SUPER CHIEF STREAMLINER: 2383 P/T A-A, 2530, 2563, 2562, and 2561.	4,000	6,500	6
2545WS: 1959 SIX-CAR N&W SPACE-FREIGHT: 746, 746W, 175, 6175, 6470, 3419, 6650, 3540, and 6517.	3,000	5,000	6
2547WS: 1960 FOUR-CAR VARIETY SPECIAL STEAM FREIGHT: 637, 2046W, 3330, 6475, 6361, and 6357.	600	1,000	5
2549W: 1960 A MIGHTY MILITARY DIESEL OUTFIT: 2349, 3540, 6470, 6819, 6650, and 3535.	1,200	2,000	3
2551W: 1960 SIX-CAR GREAT NORTHERN DIESEL FREIGHT: 2358, 6828, 3512, 6827, 6736, 6812, and 6427.	2,100	3,500	6
2553WS: 1960 THE MAJESTIC BERKSHIRE FIVE-CAR FREIGHT: 736, 2046W, 3830, 3435, 3419, 3672, and 6357.	1,500	2,500	5
2555W: 1960 OVER & UNDER TWIN RAILROAD EMPIRE: Super 0 components included: 2383P/2383T Santa Fe F3 A-A units; 6414 Evans Auto Loader; 6464-900 New York Central boxcar; 3434 operating chicken sweeper car; 3366 operating circus car; 6357-50 illuminated Santa Fe caboose. HO components included: 0565/0595 Santa Fe F3 A-A units; 0814 Evans Auto Loader; 0864-900 New York Central boxcar; 0834 illuminated poultry car; 0866-200 circus car; 0817-150 illuminated Santa Fe caboose.	8,500	40,000	8
2570: 1961 FIVE-CAR HUSKY DIESEL FREIGHT: 616, 6822, 6828, 6812, 6736, and 6130.	550	900	4
2571: 1961 FORT KNOX SPECIAL STEAM FREIGHT: 637, 736W, 3419, 6445, 6361, and 6119.	600	1,000	5
2572: 1961 FIVE-CAR SPACE AGE DIESEL FREIGHTER: 2359, 6544, 3830, 6448, 3519, and 3535.	800	1,350	4
2573: 1961 FIVE-CAR TV SPECIAL STEAM FREIGHT: 736, 736W, 3545, 6416, 6475, 6440, and 6357.	1,200	2,000	5
2574: 1961 FIVE-CAR DEFENDER DIESEL FREIGHT: 2383 P/T A-A, 3665, 3419, 448, 6448, 3830, and 6437.	1,800	3,000	5
2575: 1961 SEVEN-CAR DYNAMO ELECTRIC FREIGHT: 2360 single stripe, 6530, 6828, 6464-900, 6827, 6560, and 6437.	3,000	5,000	7
2576: 1961 FOUR-CAR SUPER CHIEF STREAMLINE: 2383 P/T A-A, 2563, 2562, 2562, and 2561.	4,000	6,500	6
3105W: 1947 ADVANCE CATALOG: 1666, 2466WX, 2452X, 2465, and 2472.	400	750	6
4109WS: 1946-47 ELECTRONIC CONTROL SET: 671R, 4671W, 4452, 4454, 5459, and 4457.	1,000	1,800	5
4110WS: 1948-49 LIONEL ELECTRONIC RAILROAD: 671R, 4671W, 4452, 4454, 5459, 4357, 97, and 151.	2,000	3,700	7

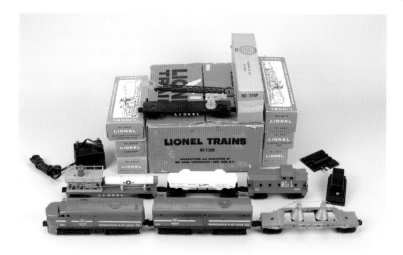

11288

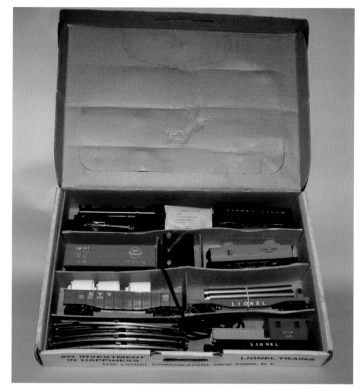

11351

	EX	LN	RARITY
11001: 1962 ADVANCE CATALOG, THREE-CAR STEAM FREIGHT: 1060, 1060T, 6402, 6042, and 6067.	75	150	3
11011: 1962 ADVANCE CATALOG, THREE-CAR DIESEL FREIGHT: 222, 6076, 3510 and 6120.	200	450	3
11201: 1962 FAST STARTER STEAM FREIGHT: 242, 1060T, 6042-75, 6502, and 6047.	90	175	1
11212: 1962 FOUR-UNIT CYCLONE DIESEL FREIGHT: 633, 3349, 6825 and 6057.	225	375	2
11222: 1962 FIVE-UNIT VAGA-BOND STEAM FREIGHT: 236, 1050T, 3357, 6343, and 6119.	125	200	3
11232: 1962 027 FIVE-UNIT DIESEL FREIGHT: 232, 3410, 6062, 6413, and 6057-50 orange.	425	700	6
11242: 1962 TRAIL BLAZER STEAM FREIGHT: 233, 233W, 6465, 6476 red, 6162, and 6017.	80	125	2
11252: 1962 027 SEVEN-UNIT DIESEL FREIGHT: 211 A-A, 3509, 6448, 3349, 6463, and 6057.	400	850	5
11268: 1962 027 SIX-UNIT DIESEL FREIGHT: 2365, 3619, 3470, 3349, 6501, and 6017.	900	1,500	4
11278: 1962 SEVEN-UNIT PLAINSMAN STEAM FREIGHT: 2037, 233W, 6473, 6162, 6050-110, 6825, and 6017.	250	450	4
11288: 1962 SEVEN-UNIT ORBITOR DIESEL FREIGHT: 229 P/C A-B, 3413, 6512, 6413, 6463, and 6059.	750	1,200	5
11298: 1962 SEVEN-UNIT VIGILANT STEAM FREIGHT: 2037, 233W, 3419, 6544, 6448, 3330, and 6017.	400	750	5
11308: 1962 027 SIX-UNIT DIESEL PASSENGER: 218 P/T A-A, 2414, two 2412s and 2416.	600	1,000	4
11311: 1963 VALUE PACKED STEAM FREIGHT: 1062, 1061T, 6409-25, 6076-100, and 6167.	90	150	2
11321: 1963 027 FIVE-UNIT DIESEL FREIGHTER: 221, 3309, 6076-75, 6042-75, and 6167-50 yellow.	250	400	3
11331: 1963 OUTDOORSMAN STEAM FREIGHT: 242, 1060T, 6473, 6476-25, 6142, and 6059-50.	125	200	2
11341: 1963 SPACE-PROBER DIESEL FREIGHT: 634, 3410, 6407, 6014-335 white, 6463, and 6059-50.	950	1,600	6
11351: 1963 LAND ROVER STEAM FREIGHT: 237, 1060T, 6050-100, 6465-100, 6408, 6162, and 6119-100.	200	350	3
11361: 1963 SHOOTING STAR DIESEL FREIGHT: 211 P/T A-A, 3665-100, 3413-150, 6470, 6413, and 6257-100.	750	1,250	6
11375: 1963 CARGOMASTER STEAM FREIGHT: 238, 234W, 6822-50, 6414-150, 6465-150, 6476-75, 6162, and 6257-100.	650	1,100	5
11385: 1963 SPACE CONQUEROR DIESEL FREIGHT: 223P/218C A-B, 3619-100, 3470-100, 3349-100, 6407, and 6257-100.	1,800	3,000	6
11395: 1963 MUSCLEMAN STEAM FREIGHT: 2037, 234W, 6464-725, 6469-50, 6536, 6440-50, 6560-50, and 6119-100.	600	1,000	5
11405: 1963 027 SIX-UNIT DIESEL PASSENGER: 218 A-A, 2414, two 2412s and 2416.	700	1,125	4

11430

11500 (Type II)

11560

	EX	LN	RARITY
11415: 1962 ADVANCE CATALOG TWO-CAR STEAM FREIGHT: 1061, 1061T, 6502 and 6167-25.	50	100	3
11420: 1964 FOUR-UNIT STEAM FREIGHT: 1061, 1061T, 6042-250 and 6167-25.	75	125	2
11430: 1964 FIVE-UNIT STEAM FREIGHT: 1062,1061T, 6176, 6142, and 6167-125.	90	150	2
11440: 1964 FIVE-UNIT DIESEL FREIGHT: 221, 3309, 6176-50 black, 6142-125 blue, and 6167-100 red.	200	350	2
11450: 1964 SIX-UNIT STEAM FREIGHT: 242, 1060T, 6473, 6142-75 green, 6176-50 black, and 6059-50.	150	250	2
11460: 1964 SEVEN-UNIT STEAM FREIGHT: 238, 234W, 6014-335 white, 6465-150 orange, 6142-100 blue, 6176-75 yellow, and 6119-100.	125	200	3
11470: 1964 SEVEN-UNIT STEAM FREIGHT: 237, 1060T, 6014-335 white, 6465-150 orange, 6142-100 blue, 6176-50 yellow, and 6119-100.	180	300	5
11480: 1964 SEVEN-UNIT DIESEL FREIGHT: 213 P/T A-A, 6473, 6176-50 black, 6142-150, 6014-335 white, and 6257-100.	600	1,000	5
11490: 1964-65 FIVE-UNIT DIESEL PASSENGER: 212 P/T A-A, 2404, 2405 and 2406.	600	1,000	4
11500 (Type I): 1964 SEVEN-UNIT STEAM FREIGHT: 2029, 234W, 6465-150 orange, 6402-50, 6176-75 yellow, 6014-335 white, and 6257-100.	250	400	4
11500 (Type II): 1965 SEVEN-UNIT STEAM FREIGHT: 2029, 234W, 6465-150 orange, 6402-50, 6176 black, 6014-335 white, and 6059.	250	400	4
11500 (Type III): 1966 SEVEN-UNIT STEAM FREIGHT: 2029, 234W, 6465-150 orange, 6402-50, 6176-75 yellow, 6014-335 white, and 6059.	250	400	4
11510: 1964 SEVEN-UNIT STEAM FREIGHT: 2029, 1060T, 6465-150 orange, 6402-50, 6176-75 yellow, 6014-335 white, and 6257-100.	275	450	4
11520: 1965-66 SIX-UNIT STEAM FREIGHT: 242, 1062T, 6176, 3364, 6142, and 6059.	100	175	2
11530: 1965-66 FIVE-UNIT DIESEL FREIGHT: 634, 6014-335 white, 6142, 6402, and 6130.	175	300	2
11540: 1965-66 SIX-UNIT STEAM FREIGHT: 239, 242T, 6473, 6465, 6176, and 6119.	175	300	5
11550: 1965-66 SIX-UNIT STEAM FREIGHT: 239, 234W, 6473, 6465, 6176, and 6119.	225	375	4
11560: 1965-66 SEVEN-UNIT DIESEL FREIGHT: 211 P/T A-A, 6473, 6176, 6142, 6465, and 6059.	250	400	2
11590: 1966 FIVE-UNIT ILLUMINATED PASSENGER: 212 P/T A-A, 2408, 2409 and 2410.	700	1,100	4
11600: 1968 SEVEN-UNIT STEAM FREIGHT: 2029, 234W, 6014-335 white, 6476 yellow, 6315, 6560, and 6130.	750	1,250	5
11710: 1969 FIVE-UNIT STEAM FREIGHT: 1061, 1062T, 6402, 6142, and 6059.	125	200	3
11720: 1969 FIVE-UNIT DIESEL FREIGHT: 2024, 6142, 6402, 6176 yellow, and 6057 brown.	200	325	5

12840

12710

	EX	LN	RARITY
11730: 1969 SIX-UNIT DIESEL FREIGHT: 645, 6402, 6014-85 orange, 6142, 6176 black, and 6167.	300	500	4
11740: 1969 SEVEN-UNIT DIESEL FREIGHT: 2041 A-A, 6315, 6142, 6014-410 white, 6476 yellow, and 6057 brown.	325	550	5
11750: 1969 SEVEN-UNIT STEAM FREIGHT: 2029, 234T, 6014-85 orange, 6476 black, 6473, 6315, and 6130.	500	800	6
11760: 1969 SEVEN-UNIT STEAM FREIGHT: 2029, 234W, 6014-410 white, 6315, 6476 black, 3376, and 6119.	300	550	4
12502: 1962 PRAIRIE-RIDER GIFT PACK: 1862, 1862T, 3376, 1877, 1866, and 1865.	600	1,100	5
12512: 1962 ENFORCER GIFT PACK: 45, 3413, 3619, 3470, 3349, and 6017.	900	1,800	5
12700: 1964 SEVEN-UNIT STEAM FREIGHT: This set was identical to the 1964 12710 listed below, but did not include a transformer.	900	1,500	5
12710: 1964 SEVEN-UNIT STEAM FREIGHT: 736, 736W, 6464-725, 6162-100 blue, 6414-75, 6476-135 yellow, and 6437.	925	1,550	5
12710: 1965-66 SEVEN-UNIT STEAM FREIGHT: 736, 736W, 6464-725, 6162-100 blue, 6414, 6476-135 yellow, and 6437.	925	1,550	5
12720: 1964 SEVEN-UNIT DIESEL FREIGHT: This set was identical to the 1964 12730 listed below, but did not include a transformer.	1,500	2,500	5
12730: 1964 SEVEN-UNIT DIESEL FREIGHT: 2383 P/T A-A, 6464-725, 6162-100 blue, 6414-75, 6476-135 yellow, and 6437.	1,500	2,500	5
12730: 1965-66 SEVEN-UNIT DIESEL FREIGHT: 2383 P/T A-A, 6464-725, 6162-100 blue, 6414, 6476-135 yellow, and 6437.	1,500	2,500	5
12740: 1964 NINE-UNIT DIESEL FREIGHT: This set was identical to the 1964 12750 listed below, but did not include a transformer.	1,500	2,500	6
12750: 1964 NINE-UNIT DIESEL FREIGHT:	Existence questioned.		
12760: 1964 NINE-UNIT STEAM FREIGHT: This set was identical to the 1964 12740 listed below, but with the diesels replaced by a steam locomotive.	1,500	2,500	6
12770: 1964 NINE-UNIT STEAM FREIGHT:	Existence questioned.		
12780: 1964-66 SIX-UNIT DIESEL PASSENGER: 2383 P/T A-A, 2523, 2522, 2523, and 2521.	3,300	5,500	5
12800: 1965-66 SIX-UNIT DIESEL FREIGHT: 2346, 6428, 6436-110, 6464-475, 6415, and 6017.	600	1,000	3
12820: 1965 EIGHT-UNIT DIESEL FREIGHT: 2322, 3662, 6822, 6361, 6464-725, 6436-110, 6315, and 6437.	1,500	2,500	5
12840: 1966 SEVEN-UNIT STEAM FREIGHT: 665, 736W, 6464-375, 6464-450, 6431, 6415, and 6437.	900	1,600	5
12850: 1966 EIGHT-UNIT DIESEL FREIGHT: 2322, 3662, 6822, 6361, 6464-725, 6436-110, 6315, and 6437.	1,500	2,500	5

13008

13108

	EX	LN	RARITY
13008: 1962 SIX-UNIT CHAMPION STEAM FREIGHT: 637, 736W, 3349, 6448, 6501, and 6119.	400	750	5
13018: 1962 SIX-UNIT STARFIRE DIESEL FREIGHT: 616, 6500, 6650, 3519, 6448, and 6017-235.	1,200	2,000	6
13028: 1962 SIX-UNIT DEFENDER DIESEL FREIGHT: 2359, 3665, 3349, 3820, 3470, and 6017-100.	900	1,500	3
13036: 1962 SIX-UNIT PLAINSMAN STEAM OUTFIT: 1872, 1872T, 6445, 3370, 1876, and 1875W.	900	1,650	4
13048: 1962 SEVEN-UNIT STEAM FREIGHT: 736, 736W, 6822, 6414, 3362, 6440, and 6437.	800	1,500	3
13058: 1962 SEVEN-UNIT VANGUARD DIESEL FREIGHT: 2383 P/T A-A, 3619, 3413, 6512, 470, 6470, and 6437.	1,600	2,700	4
13068: 1962 EIGHT-UNIT GOLIATH ELECTRIC FREIGHT: 2360 single stripe, 6464-725, 6828, 6416, 6827, 6530, 6475, and 6437.	3,000	5,000	7
13078: 1962 FIVE-UNIT PRESIDENTIAL PASSENGER: 2360 single stripe, 2523, 2522, 2522, and 2521.	3,600	6,500	6
13088: 1962 SIX-UNIT PRESIDENTIAL PASSENGER: 2383 P/T A-A, 2523, 2522, 2522, and 2521.	2,500	4,200	5
13098: 1963 GOLIATH STEAM FREIGHT: 637, 736W, 6469, 6464-900, 6414, 6446, and 6447.	2,000	3,600	6
13108: 1963 SUPER 0 SEVEN-UNIT DIESEL FREIGHT: 617, 3665, 3419, 6448, 3830, 3470, and 6119-100.	900	1,500	5
13118: 1963 SUPER 0 EIGHT-UNIT STEAM FREIGHT: 736, 736W, 6446-60, 6827, 3362, 6315-60, 6560, and 6429.	1,500	2,500	5
13128: 1963 SUPER 0 SEVEN-UNIT DIESEL FREIGHT: 2383 P/T A-A, 3619, 3413, 6512, 448, 6448, and 6437.	1,800	3,000	6
13138: 1963 MAJESTIC ELECTRIC FREIGHT: 2360 single stripe, 6464-725, 6828, 6416, 6827, 6315-60, 6436-110, and 6437.	3,000	5,000	6
13148: 1963 SUPER CHIEF PASSENGER: 2383 P/T A-A, 2523, 2523, 2522, and 2521.	2,300	4,200	5
13150 (Type I): 1964 SUPER 0 NINE-UNIT STEAM FREIGHT: 773, 736W, 3434, 6361, 3662, 6415, 3356, 6436-110, and 6437.	3,200	9,850	7
13150 (Type II): 1965-66 SUPER 0 NINE-UNIT STEAM FREIGHT: 773, 773W, 3434, 6361, 3662, 6415, 3356, 6436-110, and 6437.	3,500	11,000	7

CHRONOLOGICAL LISTING:

1945
O-GAUGE: 463W.

1946
027-GAUGE: 1400, 1400W, 1401, 1401W, 1402, 1402W, 1403, 1403W, 1405, 1405W, 1407B, 1409, 1409W, 1411W, 1413WS, 1415WS, 1417WS, 1419WS, and 1421WS.

O-GAUGE: 2100, 2100W, 2101, 2101W, 2103W, 2105WS, 2110WS, 2111WS, 2113WS, 2114WS, 2115WS, and 4109WS.

1947
027-GAUGE: 1431, 1431W, 1432, 1432W, 1433, 1433W, 1434WS, 1435WS, 1437WS, 1439WS, 1441WS, and 1443WS.

O-GAUGE: 2120S, 2120WS, 2121S, 2121WS, 2123W, 2124W, 2125WS, 2126WS, 2127WS, 2129WS, 2131WS, 3105W, and 4109WS.

1948
027-GAUGE: 1111, 1112, 1423W, 1425B, 1426WS, 1427WS, 1429WS, 1430WS, 1445WS, 1447WS, and 1449WS.

O-GAUGE: 2133W, 2135WS, 2136WS, 2137WS, 2139WS, 2140WS, 2141WS, 2143WS, 2144W, 2145WS, 2146WS, and 4110WS.

1949
027-GAUGE: 1115, 1117, 1423W, 1425B, 1426WS, 1430WS, 1447WS, 1451WS, 1453WS, 1455WS, 1457B, and 1459WS.

O-GAUGE: 2135WS, 2136WS, 2139W, 2140WS, 2141WS, 2144W, 2146WS, 2147WS, 2149B, 2151W, 2153WS, 2155WS, and 4110W.

1950
027-GAUGE: 1113, 1457B, 1461S, 1463W, 1464W, 1467W, 1469WS, 1471WS, 1473WS, and 1475WS.

O-GAUGE: 2148WS, 2150WS, 2159WS, 2161WS, 2163WS, 2165WS, 2167WS, 2169WS, 2171WS, 2173WS, 2175W, and 2185W.

1951
027-GAUGE: 1119, 1463WS, 1464W, 1467W, 1469WS, 1471WS, 1477S, and 1481WS.

O-GAUGE: 2163WS, 2167WS, 2173WS, 2175WS, and 2185WS.

1952
027-GAUGE: 1119, 1464W, 1467W, 1477S, 1479WS, 1483WS, 1484WS, and 1485WS.

O-GAUGE: 2177WS, 2179WS, 2183WS, 2187WS, 2189WS, 2190W, 2191W, and 2193W.

1953
027-GAUGE: 1464W, 1467W, 1500, 1501S, 1502WS, 1503WS, 1505WS, 1507WS, 1509WS, and 1511S.

O-GAUGE: 2190W, 2201WS, 2203WS, 2205WS, 2207W, 2209W, 2211WS, and 2213WS.

1954
027-GAUGE: 1500, 1503WS, 1513S, 1515WS, 1516WS, 1517W, 1519WS, 1520W, 1521WS, and 1523.

O-GAUGE: 2201WS, 2217WS, 2219W, 2221WS, 2222WS, 2223W, 2225WS, 2227W, 2229W, 2231W, and 2234W.

1955
027-GAUGE: 1000W, 1001, 1513S, 1525, 1527, 1529, 1531W, 1533WS, 1534W, 1535W, 1536W, 1537WS, 1538WS, 1539W, and 1541WS.

O-GAUGE: 2235W, 2237WS, 2239W, 2241WS, 2243W, 2244W, 2245WS, 2247W, 2249WS, 2251W, 2253W, and 2254W.

1956
027-GAUGE: 1542, 1543, 1545, 1547S, 1549, 1551W, 1552, 1553W, 1555WS, 1557W, 1559W, 1561WS, 1562W, 1563W, 1565WS, and 1567WS.

O-GAUGE: 2255W, 2257W, 2259W, 2261WS, 2263WS, 2265WS, 2267W, 2269W, 2270W, 2271W, 2273W, and 2274W.

1957

027-GAUGE: 1569, 1571, 1573, 1575, 1577S, 1578S, 1579S, 1581, 1583WS, 1585W, 1586, 1587S, and 1589WS.

O-GAUGE: 2275W, 2276W, 2277WS, 2279W, 2281W, 2283WS, 2285W, and 2287W.

SUPER 0: 2289WS, 2291W, 2292WS, 2293W, 2295WS, 2296W, and 2297WS.

1958

027-GAUGE: 1587S, 1590, 1591, 1593, 1595, 1597S, 1599, 1600, 1601W, 1603WS, 1605W, 1607WS, and 1608W.

SUPER 0: 2501W, 2502W, 2503WS, 2505W, 2507W, 2509WS, 2511W, 2513W, 2515WS, 2517WS, 2518W, 2519W, 2521WS, 2523W, 2525WS, and 2526W.

1959

027-GAUGE: 1105, 1609, 1611, 1612, 1613S, 1615, 1617S, 1619W, 1621WS, 1623W, 1625WS, and 1626W.

Gift Pack—no track or transformer.

1800

SUPER 0: 2527, 2528WS, 2529W, 2531WS, 2533WS, 2535WS, 2537W, 2539WS, 2541W, 2543WS, 2544W, and 2545WS.

1960

027-GAUGE: 1107, 1109, 1609, 1612, 1627S, 1629, 1631WS, 1633, 1635WS, 1637W, 1639WS, and 1640W.

Gift Pack—no track or transformer.

1800 and 1805

SUPER 0: 2527, 2528WS, 2544W, 2547WS, 2549W, 2551W, 2553WS, and 2555W.

1961

027-GAUGE: 1123, 1124, 1125, 1641, 1642, 1643, 1644, 1645, 1646, 1647, 1648, 1649, 1650, and 1651.

Gift Pack—no track or transformer.

1809 and 1810

SUPER 0: 2528WS, 2570, 2571, 2572, 2573, 2574, 2575, and 2576.

1962

027-GAUGE: 11001, 11011, 11201, 11212, 11222, 11232, 11242, 11252, 11268, 11278, 11288, 11298, and 11308.

Gift Pack—no track or transformer.

12502 and 12512

SUPER 0: 13008, 13018, 13028, 13036, 13048, 13058, 13068, 13078, and 13088.

1963

027-GAUGE: 11311, 11321, 11331, 11341, 11351, 11361, 11375, 11385, 11395, 11405, and 11415.

SUPER 0: 13098, 13108, 13118, 13128, 13138, and 13148.

1964

027-GAUGE: 11420, 11430, 11440, 11450, 11460, 11470, 11480, 11490, 11500, and 11510.

O-GAUGE: 12700, 12710, 12720, 12730, 12740, 12760, 12780, and 13150.

1965

027-GAUGE: 11490, 11500, 11520, 11530, 11540, 11550, and 11560.

O-GAUGE: 12710, 12730, 12780, 12800, and 12820.

SUPER 0: 13150.

1966

027-GAUGE: 11500, 11520, 11530, 11540, 11550, 11560, and 11590.

O-GAUGE: 12710, 12730, 12780, 12800, 12840, and 12850.

SUPER 0: 13150.

1967

In 1967, Lionel neither produced trains, nor supplied a catalog. Lionel sold only existing inventory on hand from prior years.

1968

027-GAUGE: 11600.

1969

027-GAUGE: 11710, 11720, 11730, 11740, 11750, and 11760.

Lionel Catalogs

For many, the collecting of Lionel paper goods is a hobby unto itself. Indeed, so vast was Lionel's production of trains, it is difficult to comprehend that in fact there were more different paper products produced than trains themselves. Indeed, a large display area is required to display a "complete" (whatever that means) collection of both.

Beyond the celebrated color consumer catalog, during the later portion of the prewar era, Lionel published a dealer advance catalog. Though often similar to the consumer catalog, dealer catalogs also illustrated store displays and promotional items that were not shown in the regular catalog. Also, these dealer catalogs often give us insight into how pieces evolved, for the illustrations in the dealer publication were often based on pre-production samples. Some items are shown that were never produced.

Far from the full-color 1942 catalog full of trains that closed the prewar era, the 1900 Lionel catalog was black and white, and illustrated no trains at all.

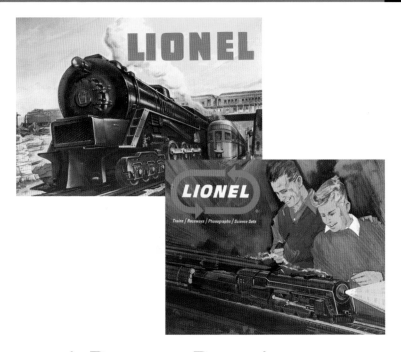

and Paper Products

Virtually every operating piece Lionel produced had its own instructional document—often several editions as production continued on good-selling items.

Booklets were printed for department store and hobby shop salespeople, teaching the "right" way to extol the virtues of Lionel's products.

Rather than trying to list and illustrate each paper product issued, which would require a massive volume, these listings will be confined to catalogs; consumer, dealer and accessory. A few other items of special interest are listed as well.

Unlike the trains, only two values are listed for paper products: Excellent and Like New. Paper in less than Excellent condition is not generally considered collectable. Beware, however, that like the trains, rare and valuable catalogs have been reproduced and those that are not marked as such are sometimes hard to distinguish.

1945 Consumer Catalog

1946 Consumer Catalog

1947 Consumer Catalog

1948 Consumer Catalog

	EX	LN	RARITY
1945 CONSUMER CATALOG: Lionel rushed an outfit on the market to meet the pent-up demand for trains caused by the war years. Only one type of outfit was available in 1945, and Lionel knew it could not meet the demand. Nevertheless, a four 8-1/2 x 11-page brochure was produced extolling the return of Lionel trains, with new features too. The company hoped to continue fanning the flames of desire among consumers until production could meet demand. The strategy worked.	150	225	8
1946 ADVANCE CATALOG: 24-page, 10-1/2 x 8-5/16 horizontal format catalog with cover reading "World's Finest Lionel Trains for 1946."	200	325	8
1946 CONSUMER CATALOG: 16-page, 8-3/8 x 11-1/4 horizontal format catalog.	40	65	6
1946 "LIBERTY" MAGAZINE: Lionel, concerned about distribution problems for their catalog, took one of the most expensive advertisements of anyone up to that time. A 16-page insert, duplicating the consumer catalog, was put in the Nov. 23, 1946 edition of "Liberty" magazine.	100	200	7
1946 SCENIC EFFECTS FOR MODEL RAILROADS: 6 x 9-inch, 24-page booklet promoting Lionel products and describing how to build a layout.	20	30	5
1947 ADVANCE CATALOG: 14 x 11-inch, 22-page vertical format catalog. The cover reads "The Lionel Line for 1947."	200	325	7
1947 CONSUMER CATALOG: Various versions of this 32-page color horizontal format catalog were printed. All were trying to get the price and description of the new GG-1 locomotive correct, and today all are equally valued.	45	80	5
1947 FUN WITH MODEL RAILROADING: 32-page booklet with red cover. This details various scenic techniques and operating ideas for a Lionel layout.	20	30	4
1948 ADVANCE CATALOG: 14 x 11-inch, 20-page horizontal format catalog. Interestingly, the new-for-1948 F-3 diesels are not shown in the advance catalog.	175	300	7
1948 CONSUMER CATALOG: 11-1/8 x 8-inch, 36-page horizontal format catalog with Pennsylvania S2 turbine on the cover.	60	80	5
1948 3-D POSTER: 18 x 19-inch red and blue printed poster of Lionel trains. Came with celluloid 3-D glasses as an insert in some of the 1948 consumer catalogs.	25	50	6
1948 MAKE THESE REALISTIC MODELS FOR YOUR LIONEL RAILROAD: 23-1/4 x 25-inch printed sheet of cut out structures printed in red, green and blue ink.	45	70	6
1948 FOR THE MAN WHO SELLS LIONEL TRAINS: This was a training booklet for Lionel retailers.	75	150	8
1949 ADVANCE CATALOG: 17 x 8-1/4-inch, 24-page horizontal format catalog.	250	400	8

1949 Consumer Catalog

1950 Consumer Catalog

1951 Consumer Catalog

1952 Consumer Catalog

1953 Consumer and
Minitature Catalogs

	EX	LN	RARITY
1949 CONSUMER CATALOG: 11-1/4 x 8-inch, 38-page horizontal format catalog. The cover illustration is of a family admiring a fantastic Lionel display. There are several minor variations of this catalog, most having to do with the 6220 locomotive on page 11, but these variations don't affect values.	150	225	7
1949 TRACK LAYOUT PLANNING BOOK FOR POP: A 16-page, 5-1/8 x 7-1/16-inch booklet of various track configurations. A pipe-smoking father figure is on the front cover.	20	35	5
1950 ADVANCE CATALOG: 11-3/8 x 8-inch horizontal format advance catalog. The cover of this catalog was gold, recognizing Lionel's 50th anniversary.	150	200	7
1950 CONSUMER CATALOG: 11-1/4 x 8-inch, 44-page horizontal format full-color catalog.	60	100	5
1950 REPLACEMENT CATALOG: This 40-page, 11 x 8-inch horizontal format catalog was issued when the supply of four-color catalogs was exhausted. It was printed in red and black ink.	100	150	7
1950 LIONEL RAILROADING IS FUN: 17-1/4 x 23-inch poster printed in green and black ink with layout ideas.	10	20	4
1951 ADVANCE CATALOG: 11 x 8-inch, 24-page advance catalog with red and black cover.	40	75	6
1951 CONSUMER CATALOG: 11-1/8 x 7-3/4-inch, 36-page horizontal format full-color catalog.	30	60	4
1951 THE ANSWER BOOK ON LIONEL TRAINS: This was a 5-1/2 x 8-1/2, 34-page training booklet for Lionel retailers.	60	80	7
1951 ROMANCE OF MODEL RAILROADING: 9 x 6-inch, 32-page orange-covered booklet lavishly illustrated with photos of the Lionel showroom layout.	15	20	3
1951 LIONEL RAILROADING IS FUN: 17-1/4 x 23-3/4-inch poster printed in blue and black ink with layout ideas.	10	20	4
1952 ADVANCE CATALOG: 11-1/8 x 8-inch, 40-page horizontal format catalog. Cover reads "Lionel Trains for 1952 Advance Catalog."	60	100	7
1952 CONSUMER CATALOG: 11-7/8 x 7-3/4, 36-page horizontal format catalog.	40	55	4
1952 LIONEL RAILROADING IS FUN: 17-1/4 x 22-3/4-inch poster printed in orange and black ink with layout ideas.	10	20	4
1952 OFFICIAL BOOK OF RULES FOR MODEL RAILROADING: 4-3/16 x 6-1/8-inch, 16-page blue-covered booklet.	15	20	4
1953 ADVANCE CATALOG: 11-1/4 x 7-5/8-inch, 44-page vertical format black and white catalog.	60	110	7
1953 CONSUMER CATALOG: 7-5/8 x 11-1/4, 40-page full-color horizontal format catalog. Two distinctly different versions of this catalog exist, but there is no difference in value.	35	60	4

1954 Consumer Catalog

1955 Consumer Catalog

1956 Consumer Catalog

1957 Consumer Catalog

1958 Consumer Catalog

	EX	LN	RARITY
1953 MINIATURE CATALOG: 7-7/8 x 5-5/8-inch, 32-page catalog with color cover and a mixture of color and black and white inside pages. Cover illustration duplicates that of the full-size consumer catalog.	20	30	5
1953 LIONEL ACCESSORIES: 9 x 6-inch, 16-page accessory catalog printed in black and red ink.	15	22	4
1954 ADVANCE CATALOG: 11-1/4 x 7-5/8-inch, 44-page horizontal format advance catalog. Cover reads "Advance Catalog 1954."	50	85	6
1954 CONSUMER CATALOG: 11-1/4 x 7-5/8-inch, 44-page horizontal format full-color catalog.	30	45	4
1954 MINIATURE CATALOG: 8-1/8 x 5-3/4-inch, 32-page catalog with color cover and black and red inside pages. Cover illustration duplicates that of the full-size consumer catalog.	20	30	5
1954 LIONEL ACCESSORIES: 9 x 6-inch, 20-page accessory catalog printed in black and green ink.	6	10	3
1954 DISTRIBUTOR'S ADVERTISING PROMOTIONS: 8-3/8 x 11-inch, 16-page privately printed black and white catalog. Made of pulp-type paper.	14	20	5
1955 ADVANCE CATALOG: 11-1/4 x 7-3/4-inch, 20-page black and white horizontal format advance catalog. The cover reads "Lionel Advance Catalog 1955..featuring Magne-traction."			
1955 ADVANCE CATALOG (Type I): Black and white cover.	30	55	6
1955 ADVANCE CATALOG (Type II): Orange, black and white cover.	35	55	6
1955 CONSUMER CATALOG: 11-1/4 x 7-5/8-inch, 44-page full-color horizontal format catalog.	25	40	3
1956 ADVANCE CATALOG: 11 x 8-inch, 48-page horizontal format black and white catalog with red, white and black cover.	60	100	7
1956 CONSUMER CATALOG: 11-1/4 x 7-5/8-inch, 40-page-full color horizontal format catalog.	30	45	3
1956 ACCESSORY CATALOG: 11 x 8-inch, 24-page horizontal format catalog printed in red and black on pulp paper.	35	50	5
1957 ADVANCE CATALOG: 11 x 8-1/4, 56-page horizontal format catalog.	100	130	7
1957 CONSUMER CATALOG: 11-1/4 x 7-1/2, 52-page full-color horizontal format catalog.	20	30	4
1957 ACCESSORY CATALOG: 10 x 7-1/2, 32-page horizontal format catalog printed on pulp paper.	10	15	5
1957 HO CATALOG: 10-7/8 x 7-5/8, four-page color brochure.	10	15	5
1958 ADVANCE CATALOG: 10-7/8 x 8-1/4, 64-page horizontal format catalog.	35	60	6
1958 CONSUMER CATALOG: 11-1/4 x 7-5/8-inch, 56-page full-color horizontal format catalog.	18	25	4

1959 Consumer Catalog

1960 Consumer Catalog

1961 Consumer Catalog (Type I)

1961 Consumer Catalog (Type II)

1962 Consumer Catalog

1963 Consumer Catalog

	EX	LN	RARITY
1958 ACCESSORY CATALOG: 11-1/8 x 8-inch, 32-page horizontal format catalog printed on pulp paper.	10	15	5
1958 HO CATALOG: Six-page full-color horizontal format brochure.	10	15	5
1959 ADVANCE CATALOG: 8-1/2 x 10-7/8-inch, 44-page vertical format catalog.	25	40	5
1959 CONSUMER CATALOG: 11 x 8-1/2-inch, 56-page full-color horizontal format catalog.	18	25	4
1959 ACCESSORY CATALOG: 8 x 11-inch, 36-page vertical format catalog printed on pulp paper.	10	15	5
1959 HO CATALOG: 8 x 10-7/8-inch, eight-page vertical format color catalog.	10	15	5
1960 ADVANCE CATALOG: 8-1/2 x 11-inch, 60-page vertical format catalog.	20	30	4
1960 CONSUMER CATALOG: 8-3/8 x 11-inch, 56-page full-color horizontal format catalog.	14	20	3
1960 ACCESSORY CATALOG: 8-5/8 x 11-inch, 36-page vertical format catalog printed on pulp paper.	6	10	5
1960 HO CATALOG: 8-1/2 x 10-7/8-inch, 12-page vertical format color catalog.	6	10	5
1961 ADVANCE CATALOG: 8-1/2 x 11-inch, 76-page vertical format catalog.	30	45	6
1961 CONSUMER CATALOG (Type I): 8-1/2 x 11-inch, 72-page full-color vertical format catalog printed on coated stock.	14	20	3
1961 CONSUMER CATALOG (Type II): 8-1/2 x 11-inch, 56-page vertical format catalog printed on pulp paper.	12	20	5
1962 ADVANCE CATALOG: 8-1/2 x 11-inch, 64-page vertical format catalog.	30	45	6
1962 LIONEL-SPEAR-TRI-ANG ADVANCE CATALOG: 8-3/8 x 11-inch, 55-page vertical format catalog.	15	25	5
1962 CONSUMER CATALOG: 8-1/2 x 11-inch, 100-page full-color vertical format catalog printed on coated stock. Includes slot cars and science products.	14	20	3
1962 ACCESSORY CATALOG: 8-3/8 x 10-7/8-inch, 40-page vertical format catalog printed on pulp paper.	6	10	5
1962 LIONEL TRACK LAYOUTS: 8-3/8 x 11-inch, four-page brochure showing track layouts in 027, Super 0 and HO-Gauges.	8	12	5
1962 PROMOTIONAL LITERATURE: 8-1/2 x 11-inch, four-page brochure entitled "Planning Guide to Setting Up Your Lionel Trains and Accessory Department."	25	40	6
1963 ADVANCE CATALOG: 8-1/2 x 11-inch, 80-page vertical format catalog.	50	85	7
1963 CONSUMER CATALOG: 8-3/8 x 10-7/8-inch, 56-page vertical format catalog printed with full-color cover. Includes slot cars and science products.	7	12	3

1964 Consumer Catalog
(Types I & II)

1965 Consumer Catalog
(Types I & II)

1966 Consumer Catalog

1968 Consumer Catalog

1969 Consumer Catalog

	EX	LN	RARITY
1963 ACCESSORY CATALOG: 8-3/8 x 10-7/8-inch, 40-page vertical format catalog printed on pulp paper.	6	10	5
1963 SCIENCE CATALOG: 8-3/8 x 10-7/8-inch, 32-page vertical format catalog printed on pulp paper.	6	10	5
1964 CONSUMER CATALOG (Type I): 8-1/2 x 11-inch, 24-page vertical format catalog printed on coated stock.	9	14	3
1964 CONSUMER CATALOG (Type II): 8-1/2 x 11-inch, 24-page vertical format catalog printed on pulp paper.	11	18	3
1965 CONSUMER CATALOG (Type I): 8-1/2 x 10-7/8-inch, 40-page vertical format catalog printed on coated stock. Includes slot cars and science products.	11	18	3
1965 CONSUMER CATALOG (Type II): 8-1/2 x 10-7/8-inch, 40-page vertical format catalog printed on pulp paper. Includes slot cars and science products.	9	14	3
1966 ADVANCE CATALOG: 9-7/8 x 8-1/2, 40-page full-color horizontal format catalog.	140	200	8
1966 CONSUMER CATALOG: 10-7/8 x 8-3/8-inch, 40-page full-color horizontal format catalog.	10	15	3
1966 WELCOME TO THE WONDERFUL WORLD OF LIONEL TRAINS: Single 8-1/2 x 21-3/4-inch sheet brochure folded to 3-1/2 x 8-1/2 inches.	5	8	5
1967	NO CATALOG ISSUED		
1968 ADVANCE PRODUCT SHEET: A far cry from the thick advance catalogs of just a few years earlier, this single 8-1/2 x 11-inch white card showed in blue what was to be the 1968 product line.	10	16	7
1968 CONSUMER CATALOG: 8-1/2 x 11-inch, eight-page vertical format full color catalog.	8	12	3
1969 ADVANCE CATALOG: 11 x 8-1/2-inch eight-page horizontal format catalog.	25	40	7
1969 CONSUMER CATALOG: 11 x 8-1/2-inch eight-page full-color horizontal format catalog.	10	15	3

How To Clean and Prepare Trains for Use After Long-Term Storage

In the instruction booklet Lionel furnished with their outfits in the 1950s it was recommended to customers that they keep all the original packaging materials to protect the trains during storage or travel. Oftentimes however that was not the case, and the boxes went outside or in the fireplace Christmas morning.

In the passing years trains were stored in attics, basements, closets, oftentimes in no box at all. Dust and dirt filter into the working mechanisms of the trains as well as coating the shiny finish Lionel carefully applied to their bodies. Stored in hot attics, lubricants solidified in solid blocks. In damp basements humidity allowed rust to work its evil on plated or blackened surfaces and on wheels once worn shiny from use.

If it is your intention to sell your trains to a collector or dealer wholesale, then it is my recommendation that you do not attempt to clean the trains. The dealer or collector knows how to clean each piece without damage and can tell even in a dirty state how the item will clean up and what it will be worth. He will pay slightly less for a dirty piece to recoup his time. However, inappropriate cleaning easily damages certain trains and once the damage

is done, the value is permanently diminished. Better that you allow the dealer to do the clean up than for you to take this risk.

If you are keeping the trains for yourself and want to clean them up, what follows are a few general tips.

The first thing that most people notice needs cleaning is the track. Do NOT use steel wool or sandpaper to clean the track. Steel wool will deposit fine metal fibers that will cause short circuits and sandpaper will remove the tinplating that protects the track from further rust. Excellent results can be had with 3-M "Scotchbrite" pads available in auto parts stores. Various textures are available. These non-metallic pads make short work of dirt and light rust deposits, especially the courser textures. While the entire exposed surface of the connecting pins needs to be clean, only the tops of the rails require thorough cleaning.

If the train is painted red, it is my recommendation that you do no more than dust it off. If you feel more thorough cleaning is required, consult "The Standard Catalog of® Lionel Trains, 1945-69."

Lionel's trains were well-made, reliable toys; often they will work as well today as the day they were made. However there are some simple steps you should take to protect the trains, and more importantly you and your family, before plugging in the toys you just hauled down from the attic or home from a garage sale.

The instructions below serve two purposes. They will aid failing memories in the event the train's original instructions have been lost or discarded. They also contain some tips necessary due to the age of the trains. Remember, when Lionel wrote their instruction sheets, they were for use with new toys!

First, and absolutely most importantly, examine the transformer (power pack), if it has been exposed to an obvious roof leak, or has a broken or cracked case, take it into a qualified Lionel service man before proceeding. Next, grasp the power cord and bend it 180

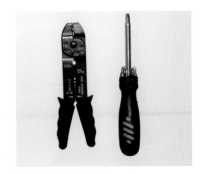

degrees, tightly. If the insulation cracks or breaks off, the transformer needs service. This is a common problem, and the transformer is the only area with much potential for injury. Do not be tempted to wrap the cord in electrical tape or to splice on a new wire. Lionel knotted their power cords inside the transformer case to act as a strain relief, and the insulation there will be failing if the insulation you can see is failing.

Next, examine the visible wiring on the underside of illuminated or operating cars such as steam locomotive tenders, cabooses, passenger cars or unloading freight cars. Make sure that none of the tiny wire leads have broken loose, and that the insulation on those leads is still intact and pliable.

Should you choose to permanently attach your train's track to a board, don't do this until it has been test run, and then use screws, not nails to attach the track. Nails work loose, and a misplaced hammer blow can permanently deform the rails. Even at this, based on the author's years of experience in the hobby shop industry, if the train is for a child, resist the urge to fasten the track to a sheet of plywood—this in essence is the same as gluing together Legos. The creativity, as well as the ability to expand the railroad stops when the track is screwed down. From then on the child is destined to only watch the train circle round a sheet of plywood, and hence will lose interest rapidly.

Once you have your track sections connected together, attach the wires to the end and then the lockon to the track as shown in figure here. Before placing the trains on the track, plug the transformer into a wall outlet. If your transformer is equipped with lights, the green one should now glow, and the red one, if so equipped should be off. On transformers equipped with a red light, it indicates that the circuit breaker has opened due to a short circuit. Advance the throttle again watching for a change in any indicator lights, a dimming green light or glowing red light is a sign of a short circuit. If your transformer has no lights, it should emit a pleasant hum when plugged in, a clicking is a sign of a short circuit.

Using a pair of wire strippers, carefully remove a short section of the insulation from each end of the hook up wire.

Depress the end of one fahnstock clip on the lockon and slip the end of the wire through to SMALL lock. Releasing the end of the clip locks it in place. Repeat the process with the second wire and the other fahnstock clip, ensuring that not even a single strand of wire touches between the two clips.

The UTC universal lockon can be used with either Standard- or O-Gauge track.

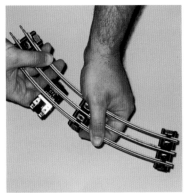

Place the bar beneath the word "LOCKON" over the lower flange of the outer rail, the tab above the word "LIONEL" will now snap over the opposite flange of the center rail. The lockon will now be securely in place. The lockon can be attached to any section off track, curved or straight.

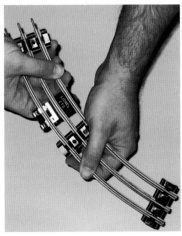

This is how NOT to attach a lockon. This is the number one mistake made in the initial set up. If hooked up like this, not only will the train not run, if allowed to remain this way, serious damage to the transformer can occur.

Glossary

AAR: Association of American Railroads, a full-sized railroad industry standards and lobbying group.

Bakelite: A brand of hard, brittle thermoset plastic. Heating Bakelite does not soften it, making it popular for electrical components. Lionel also used Bakelite occasionally for car bodies.

Cupola: The raised structure on the roof of a caboose that allowed a clear view of the sides of the train, making dragging equipment and "hot boxes" easily spotted regardless of the height of the remainder of the train.

Die-casting: A manufacturing process that involves forcing molten metal, usually a zinc alloy, into a mold, called a die, under high pressure. Rugged, detailed, precisely made parts can be mass-produced in this manner.

E-unit: This has two meanings. A) In Lionel trains, the electromechanical switch that selects motor contacts, and thus the motor's direction of rotation, is called an "E-unit." It is usually cycled by interrupting the current flow to the track. These come in two-position (forward-reverse) or three-position versions, as well as a manual version that is two-position, but requires hands-on operation by the operator. Three-position E-units are the most common, and their sequence of operation is forward-neutral-reverse-neutral-forward. B) In real railroading, E-unit is slang for a General Motors Electro-Motive Division E-series twin-engine diesel that rode on two A-1-A trucks. The two terms are not generally confused, as Lionel did not build a miniature E-unit locomotive during the prewar era.

Gauge: The distance between the tops of the rails. On most real U.S. railroads, this is 4', 8-1/2". For Lionel's most popular size of trains, this width is 1-1/4".

Heat stamping: A decorating process in which a heated die is used to transfer and adhere colored decoration to the subject piece. When used on plastics, heat stamping often leaves an impression, the depth of which varies with the temperature of the tool and the duration of contact. When used on painted sheet metal components, the underlying paint is occasionally softened, and thus the stamping can sometimes be felt.

Hot box: Early railroad wheel bearings were lubricated with oil-soaked cotton called "waste." These bearings, or journals, as well as the "waste," were housed in journal boxes. If the lubrication ran dry, the bearing would overheat, setting fire to the waste. If the train continued to operate, the bearing would fail, derailing the train.

House car: This standard railroad industry term is used for enclosed freight cars such as box, stock, refrigerator and poultry cars. These cars are used for lading requiring protection from weather, and the construction of these cars rather resembled that of a house.

Journal box: The enclosure at the junction of the axle and truck sideframe, which housed the axle bearing, or journal, and the cotton waste that acted as a lubricant reservoir.

Lithography: A printing process often used on metal surfaces. Part of the surface is treated to retain ink while other areas are treated to repel ink. This process allows elaborate and colorful decorations to be applied.

Rubber stamping: A decorating process that uses an engraved rubber block, which is inked then pressed to the subject. Rubber stamping tends to not be as bold, or as permanent, as heat stamping. However, rubber-stamping can be used on irregular surfaces which heat stamping cannot, and the set-up cost is considerably less.

Scale: A numeric ratio describing the relative size of a miniature to an original.

Silk screening: A labor-intensive decorating process. A piece of sheer fabric (originally silk, now polyester) is stretched tight. A thin sheet of plastic, with holes cut out to reveal where ink is to appear on the work piece, is placed over the screen. The screen is pressed to the work piece ink, then forced through the openings in the plastic, and through the screen onto the work surface. Multi-color designs require multiple screens, and the inks are applied sequentially starting with the lightest color and moving up to the darkest.

Sintered Iron: Sintering is a metallurgical process in which powdered metal is poured into a mold and subjected to heat and pressure, thus forming it into a single part.

Tack board: Wooden panels on an otherwise steel door provided a place to attach various notes.

Truck: The structure consisting of paired wheels with axles, side frame, bolster and suspension system beneath railroad cars. This is referred to as a "bogie" in Europe.

NATIONAL TRAIN MUSEUM

HEADQUARTERS FOR THE
TRAIN COLLECTORS ASSOCIATION

Many of the trains shown in this volume are from the collection of the National Toy Train Museum, headquarters for The Train Collectors Association. The TCA is an international organization of men and women dedicated to collecting and preserving toy trains.

The Train Collectors Association, was born from a 1954 meeting in the Yardley, Pennsylvania barn of Ed Alexander. The TCA has grown to nearly 32,000 members today. A national office, along with a museum, was built in Strasburg, Pennsylvania to accommodate the growing needs. The building has undergone 3 expansions since that time.

Toy trains are presented in a colorful and exciting turn-of-the-century setting. The Museum's vast collection of floor toys, electric trains and train-related accessories includes those from the mid-1800s through the present. See Lionel, American Flyer, Marx, Marklin, LGB and many, many others.

The National Toy Train Museum offers five operating layouts: Standard, "0", "S", "G" and HO gauges. The Standard gauge layout highlights tinplate trains from the 1920s and 1930s. The "0" gauge layout presents trains from the 1940s through current production items. The "S" gauge layout highlights American Flyer trains manufactured during the 1950s. The "G" gauge layout shows what one can do with large, durable modern trains which are made for indoor or outdoor use. The HO gauge layout was professionally built by Carstens Publications, Inc. for a series of articles published in its Railroad Model Craftsman magazine.

A continuously running video show in The Museum's Theater area features cartoons and comedy films about toy trains. The Museum Gift Shop offers a wide and unusual selection of toy train-related gifts. Also

housed in the Museum is an extensive Toy Train Reference Library, which is open to the public. On file are catalogs, magazines and books devoted to toy trains from 1900 to the present.

Come to Strasburg and visit the National Toy Train Museum where we have 5 different gauge layouts operating and displays of trains dating from 1840 until the present. If you are a person with a few trains or a house full, come join us.

OPEN:
- Weekends in April, November and December
- Daily — May through October
- 10:00 a.m. - 5:00 p.m.

visit their website at

www.traincollectors.org

for additional information.

Many of the photos in this volume were provided by Stout Auctions, one of the nation's premier toy train auctioneers. Located in both Williamsport, Ind. and West Middlesex, Pa. Stout specializes in liquidating collections of premium quality trains, including the previous owner of Lionel and other high profile individuals. Stout currently has many record auction items including one of the most important toy trains ever sold—the brass Lionel 700E scale Hudson that sat in Joshua Lionel Cowen's office. Consigned items are offered for both on-site and Internet bidding. For more information call 765-764-6901, or visit www.stoutauctions.com.

Keep Your Toy Train Knowledge Current

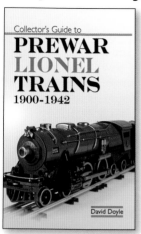

Collector's Guide to Prewar Lionel Trains, 1900-1942
by David Doyle

This fact-packed toy train guide fits in your back pocket, and contains numerically arranged listings for 2,000 models of prewar Lionel trains, including 2-7/8-Gauge, Standard, O-Gauge, OO-Gauge and accessories. Never again be without the values and identifying details you need to make the most of every train show, and visit to the hobby shop.

Softcover • 5 x 8 • 272 pages
1,000 color photos
Item# Z0725 • $19.99

Collector's Guide to Classic O-Gauge Trains
by David Doyle

Compact enough to carry to shows and shops, and more complete in production details and collector values than any other guide, *Collector's Guide to Classic O-Gauge Trains* is your must-have toy train guide. With rarity rating information, detailed descriptions and reliable collector values, you get all you need for less than $20!

Softcover • 5 x 8 • 272 pages
1,000+ color photos
Item# Z0724 • $19.99

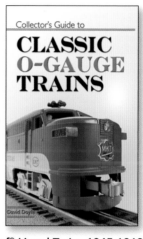

Standard Catalog of® Lionel Trains 1945-1969
2nd Edition
by David Doyle

Everything you need for successful Lionel train collecting is in this book. With 1,450 vibrant color photos, current collector pricing, rarity ratings and tips for maintaining and repairing trains, you'll have the world of postwar Lionel at your fingertips.

Softcover • 8-1/4 x 10-7/8 • 400 pages
1,450 color photos
Item# Z0096 • $32.99

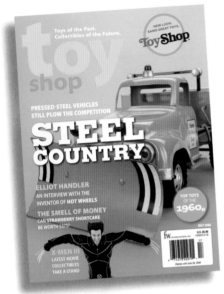